OMEGA DYNAMICS
STUDY GUIDE

Jamie Walden

Cover design and interior formatting by:

King's Custom Covers
www.KingsCustomCovers.com

Omega Dynamics
Name, Logo and Lion & Swords Crest;
Copyright © 2019 Walden Dynamics

For more information contact:
jamiewalden@omegadynamics.org

Or visit:
www.omegadynamics.org

ISBN-13: 978-1794548916

First Edition: February 2019

10 9 8 7 6 5 4 3 2 1

Contents

About the Author

Jamie Walden is the author of a the powerfully refreshing and insightful book, *OMEGA DYNAMICS: EQUIPPING A WARRIOR CLASS OF CHRISTIANS FOR THE DAYS AHEAD*. As a Marine Corps Infantry Sergeant, Police Officer, Firefighter/ Paramedic Specialists, Tactical Medic, and Disaster Response Specialist turned Missionary, researcher, and writer, Jamie uses his experiences and command of Biblical Truth to take Christians from the "Recruiters Office" to top-tier warriors. His tenacity and zeal for Christ Jesus have impassioned him with a devotion to strengthen, equip, and challenge a *"WARRIOR CLASS"* of Christians to *ARISE* and take their places as Victors in this generation. Jamie currently lives in Iowa with his wife and three children.

Jamie Walden is a powerful speaker for any audience across a wide variety of subjects effecting the Church. From Prophetic Trends & Analysis to renewing our identity in Christ Jesus as Warriors in a Kingdom that cannot be shaken, Jamie addresses the topics the Body of Christ desperately need to hear.

Contact Jamie Walden at:
jamiewalden@omegadynamics.org

Or visit:
www.omegadynamics.org

Introduction

"...we are given charge by our Holy Commander-in-Chief to be bold, steadfast, fixated, and prepared for action. We are to be mighty conquerors on the offensive who operate from a rich intimacy and "knowing" of our Commander-in-Chief under Whose Banner we fight. The True and Better Conquering King, Christ Jesus, is already established as both our Perfect example on which to fix our eyes, and our Perfect substitute in our wayward failings. His power, His strength, His authority and victory, His love, His promises and the light of His face are the hallmarks of the Ethos of the Warrior Class of the Most High in this generation. These are the attributes of the Warrior Culture to which 'those with ears to hear' have henceforth been called." [Omega Dynamics, p. 4]

The world around us is changing with unfathomable intensity and velocity. Some of us assume a posture of apathy and indifference; this yields increasing compromise and delusion. Some of us are *awake* to the threats and long to stand for truth, righteousness, and the glory of King Jesus in this generation; this yields many questions in need of answers:

 What does the future hold in light of such radical changes occurring all around us?

 I'm in a War? How do I understand the nature of this war?

 What is my position to play in this increasingly hostile environment?

 How do I truly become a Warrior for the Lord God Almighty?

 What does it mean to "know" the Lord and "do exploits" in this generation?

 How do I stand firm amid all of the competing voices, deceptions, threats, and chaos?

 How do I fight against physical and spiritual onslaught taking place all around us?

 Who will be standing to my right and to my left in the days ahead?

 What are my weapons of warfare so I can withstand in this generation?

 How do I cling to hope, joy, and thanksgiving in such a darkening world?

The book, *Omega Dynamics*, along with this Study Guide, serve to sow the seeds of our marvelous, unshakeable identities as *literal* Warriors in a *literal* war. This is a war being waged for the souls of men, to the subterfuge of our joy and communion with the Father, and against the glory of the Lord Most High; but it is also a war in which we have been assured *consummate Victory*! Therefore, it is time to harrow the fallow ground of our understanding in order to make way for the abundant cultivation of *freedom, courage, boldness, steadfastness*, and an *Authentic, Conquering Love* for both King and Brother.

> *"The Lord's intent through Creation, and in particular humanity, was that He would be fully known and glorified. Hence why you and I were eternally created; because that is exactly how long it will take to fully come to know Him! He invites us to search out the things of His Kingdom. He invites us to know Him with rich intimacy while simultaneously demonstrating the reciprocally rich intimacy of His longing to know us. He, in great wisdom and righteousness, has written each and every one of us into the battle that rages against His glory and against our identity. The Lord has determined that we are to be co-Operators with Him in the war. It is because of this that the people of God must get trained and equipped to engage in the fight (O.D., p. 14)."*

Through the strategic actions of a Cosmic Insurgency our *IDENTITIES* as Warriors and Soldiers amongst the ranks of the Lord of the Heaven's Armies have been maligned, usurped, and all together destroyed (Ps. 11:3). Therefore, we *must* approach this *STUDY GUIDE* with a sincere desire to **learn**; or as the Apostle Paul aptly states, "[to] abound more and more in knowledge and depth of insight so that you may be able to discern what is best and may be pure and blameless for the Day of Christ, filled with the fruit of righteousness that comes through Jesus Christ—to the glory and praise of God (Phil 1:9-11, Col 1:9-14, Eph 1:3-22).

Christ Jesus Himself, our soon-coming Conquering King, *has* assessed the attrition of our combat zone:

> *"When He [Jesus] saw the crowds, He had compassion for them, because they were harassed and helpless, like sheep without a shepherd. Then He said to His disciples, 'The harvest is plentiful, but the laborers are few; therefore* **pray earnestly** *to the Lord of the harvest to send out laborers into his harvest (Matt 9:35-38).'"*

It is therefore the mandate of "those with ears to hear" to "Make Ready" for the "Baptism of Fire" by the Holy Spirit, "Purify our Camps", solidify our hearts and minds in the victory of Christ Jesus, and march out within the ranks of the Warrior Redeemed during this time "such as has not been from the beginning of the world until now, no, and never will be" (Matt 24:21). In a deep *knowing* of our Warrior King, we are to advance unto great exploits in the blessed Mission of bringing in the Great Harvest (Dan 11:32)!

As we appropriate the richness of the love of the Captain of our Salvation (John 15:13), the overwhelming provision of Force Multipliers in the Holy Spirit (1 Cor 1:4-9), and an increased confidence in the light of God's face that shines upon us (Ps 44:3-8), our identity as *confident*, *secure*, *effectual*, and *worshipful* "Door-Kickers" will burst forth (2 Cor 10:3-5).

The Training Ground

This *Study Guide* is analogous to a *Military Training Evolution*. As we learn the depths and wonders of our *inherited* Heavenly Warrior Culture, we will begin to seize upon the True and Better Warrior Mindset. **This Guide will walk us through the following:**

1. "YOU DON'T' KNOW WHAT YOU DON'T KNOW"

[Acts 8:27-31, Heb 5:11-14, Josh 1:8, 2 Tim 3:1-7]

- Threat, what threat? War, what war? Role, what role would I possibly have to play?
- A Christian is to be a Warrior? How do I stand as a Warrior; I am the *least* among men?

2. "YOU TRAIN HOW YOU FIGHT AND YOU FIGHT HOW YOU TRAIN"

[Acts 17:11, Isa 26:9, Ps 119:120, Ps 73:25, Ps. 63:1, Matt 5:6]

- I *long* for more; more of Christ Jesus, more of the Word, more renewal, growth, equipping, etc.
- Blessed be the LORD, my rock, who trains my hands for war, and my fingers for battle (Ps 144:1)

3. "I AM A WARRIOR, THAT IS WHO I AM!"

[Isa 51:1, Heb 5:14, 2 Tim 2:15, Ps. 73:26, Rev 1:3]

- I look toward the rock from which I was cut, the quarry from which I was hewn!
- The power of the Gospel of Jesus Christ is alive and well in me!
- My weapons of warfare are not carnal, but *mighty* to tearing down of strongholds (2 Cor 10:4,5)!
- Greater is He Who is in me than he who is in the world (1 John 4:4).
- The Lord is on my side; I will not fear. What can man do to me (Ps 118:6)? The Lord is

my light and my salvation—whom shall I fear? The Lord is the stronghold of my life—of whom shall I be afraid (Ps 27)? How the oppressor has come to an end! How his fury has ended (Isa 14:4)!

4. "<u>GET ME IN THE FIGHT!</u>"

- I have a *knowing* of you, Lord: "With God we shall do valiantly; it is He Who will tread down our foes (Ps 60:12)!"

- My heart is secure, steadfast, and full of praise (Ps 112)!

- As you, Christ Jesus, overcame (John 16:33), so too will I get in the fight and overcome!

Moreover, our Task and Purpose is to **<u>learn</u>**! We must *learn* (or perhaps *renew*) the basis for our hope, power, authority, and mission-set in this generation! We must learn the weapons, confidence, and competence with which we conduct our far-superior Counter Insurgency against all Enemies *both foreign and domestic*. We must learn our radical, marvelous identity as love-compulsed Warrior Sons and Daughters who are mighty through God the Father, Christ the Son, and the Holy Spirit!

WORKING THROUGH THIS GUIDE

This *Study Guide* is designed to be used in conjunction with the book, *Omega Dynamics: Equipping a Warrior Class of Christians for the Days Ahead*. Whether being utilized for intimate, individual growth, or in a small-group, church development, or ministry-based teaching/training, it will serve to sharpen our Swords and consecrate our camps (Josh 7). As we do so, we begin to stand in the calling for which we have been foreknown (Isa 60:1-3, Eph 5:8-16, Rev 12:11), fellowship with renewed intimacy (John 13:34, I John 1), and grow our roots down deep into our immovable identity in Christ Jesus (Jer 17:7-8, Rev 2:25-29). In this, we make much of Christ Jesus, the Captain of our Salvation, as we simultaneously strike a blow against *all* Enemies of the Glory of God!

<u>AS YOU ADVANCE ON THE BATTLEFIELD, REMEMBER:</u>

- **BE BEREAN**: You will only get out of this what you are willing to put into it; study to show yourself a workman approved.

- **PRAY CONTINUALLY**: Ask the Lord to reveal intensely, expose intimately, and edify immensely as you seek to *know* Him and to be *known* by Him.

- **REJOICE OFTEN:** Extol the Lord for His mercy to tear down and to build up; praise Him for the *Good News* of your identity as the Warrior Redeemed in a Kingdom that cannot be shaken!

- **SHARPEN YOUR SWORD:** *READ* the multitude of Scriptural References in both the book and the Study Guide. It is the mighty Weapon which you have been commanded to *take* (Eph 6:17)! And it is the weapon which will never pass away (Matt 24:35)!

- **GROW IN A *KNOWING* OF YOUR GOD:** The Lord has a Mission for you in this generation; a Mission to be among those who *overcome* (Rev 2&3). The harvest is plentiful, the workers are few (Luke 10:2)! Redeem the time, for the days are evil (Eph 5:16)!

- **STAND UP, WARRIOR:** Move out from *His* power, *His* ability, *His* strength, *His* provision, *His* victory, and the light of *His* face, because He loves us!

NOTES

SESSION 1

Battlefield Assessment

This is the war we are in, Beloved! Our churches, Pulpits, homes, hearts, and minds are the battlefield! Battles are not fought over a difference of opinion or slight deviation of interest; they are fought because of gross offenses, because terrible casualties have been incurred, and because some great strategic loss or gain is to be made. It is to our great strategic gain that we throw off our "invalid assumptions" and with integrity assess our critical vulnerabilities in order to shore up our defenses, strengthen our feeble minds, and then aggrandize and exploit our overwhelming tactical advantages through Christ Jesus against the Enemy!

*We must test ourselves and one another in matters of the Kingdom; not as a matter of fault-finding, superiority, condemnation, or haughtiness, **but out of a sincere love for each other's standing before Christ** (1 John 4:1, 2 Cor 13:5, Rev 2:2, 1 John 2:3-6). We must have a confident, unwavering and uncompromising zeal for our Commander-in-Chief, the Captain of our Salvation, and the ranks of Heaven's Armies into which we have been conscripted.*

As we employ these things, we begin to act as a Body, as a Warrior Class, rightly discerning the great things of God. We dynamically war against those Rebel Forces within and without. Let it never be said of us that we marched into battle bewildered and unarmed (lacking the Sword of the Spirit, the Word of God). Let it never be said of us that we "died" during the most horrific wartime famine in human history, the famine of "hearing the Word of God" (Amos 8:11-12). The time has come for a Warrior Culture to arise, purify our camps, take up Arms (the Word and our Identity in Christ), and liberate Enemy-held territory in power, love, and soundness of mind! Our D-Day is upon us, therefore, "Prepare to March"! (O.D., p. 37-39)

1. **Page 8 states**, "The first endeavor taken prior to any combat engagement is the thorough assessment of both the menacing threat demanding action, as well as your personal readiness to undertake that action. It is no different with the 'Kingdom Reality' of God's *cosmic* theater of war as established from Genesis to Revelation: The 'Bad News' must be understood before being able to fully comprehend the 'Good News.'"

Take some time to focus on your personal "*Capabilities Assessment*" as it currently stands: Analyze the threats facing you personally and those facing the Church as a whole. Also, analyze your readiness to confront these threats *emotionally*, *physically*, and *spiritually*.

THREATS (Where Confrontation is Occurring)	CRITICAL VULNERABILITIES (My Vulnerabilities to the Threats)	CENTER OF GRAVITY (My Ability to Confront the Threats)

2. **Using Scripture,** identify the "*Bad News*" confronting creation (in the natural, the supernatural, internal, external, prophetically, eternally, etc.). Again, using Scripture, list the "Good News" for all creation, and in particular humanity, using the same guidelines:

3. **Page 10 admonishes,** "The error of 'assumption' or 'presumption' on a field of battle is catastrophic! Walking casually down a city street where it is 'presumed' there are no more Enemy Insurgents is often a regrettable choice. Similarly, it would be an exceptionally regrettable choice to 'presume' that simply because we bear the name 'Christian' we can stroll in oblivion through Enemy-held territory unscathed.

List several "invalid assumptions, inaccurate stereotypes, and erroneous capabilities assessments" (p. 10) that are being held by the Church with regard to Spiritual Warfare, Cultural Warfare, and the war for the eternal souls of men, defining our role in it. [**Example**: We're "doing it", look at our numbers in the church; I don't have to worry, I won't be here anyway; war, what war?; there is nothing I can do about it; those *things* are a distraction from the Gospel; hey, "*love wins*"; Jesus is sovereign over all, therefore we don't have a role; I'll just have faith when I need it; I prayed the sinner's prayer so I'm good-to-go; its prophetic, nothing I can do about it; we are only called to *love well*, etc.]

1. _____

2. _____

3. _____

4. _____

5. _____

4. **Page 13 states,** "Where the Bugler's Call (i.e. the Pulpit) is errant, absent, or faulty, where there is ambiguity or uncertainty, there you will find chaos."

What are the effects of hearing a *faulty trumpet blast* amid a battle? How does it impact the Church and Its mission to *know* the Lord and make Him *known* (p. 11-14)?

5. **"Ignorance (often laden with hubris)** is like a deeply laid mine-field that cripples any attempts of advancing on the battlefield…"

Page 16: "To this end, the _____ _____ of ignorance among the People of God are the same as any other mind-altering drug: _____, _____, _____ reality, _____ judgment, _____ vision, delayed or _____ reactions, and a *fleeting*, _____ sense of joy!"

6. <u>Read</u>: Ezekiel 22:26, James 4:4, Revelation 3:17-19, Deuteronomy 8:10-20, Haggai 1:5-11, Hosea 9:7-8, Isaiah 8:13-14, 2 Timothy 4:1-4

Why do many churches/Christians *willfully* and *deliberately* choose ignorance in this particular Church Age (ignorance of the Word, righteousness, eternal-perspective, Fear of the Lord, threats and trends, wisdom and understanding, etc.)? In what areas have you *deliberately* chosen to be ignorant, a skeptical-scoffer, or a *willful-ostrich* about the world around you, and why?

7. **One of the most defining characteristics** of the last Church Age is Its *faulty self-actualization*; Its inability/unwillingness to acknowledge Its true condition before a Holy God.

<u>Read the Scriptures on Pages 22-25</u>:

a. **God has requirements for His Warrior Class. Does your personal conduct (family, home, ambitions, entertainment, finances, focus, church activities, etc.) align with them? Does the conduct and focus of your church and Church Body?**

b. How are you and your church distinguishable from the world surrounding it?

  [i.e. If you were brought to court for being a Christian, would there be enough evidence to convict you?]

c. How is a reduction, removal, or altering of the Word of the Lord from the Pulpit a strategic act of warfare by the Enemy? What is *the Enemy's* overall mission (*their* tactical advantage) by doing so?

8. **"The Church is languishing** because by and large it does not know the truth, the truth is not presented unashamedly in its totality, and at the same time, the people vehemently oppose the truth and sound teaching even where it is presented to them. It therefore can come as no surprise that lawlessness abounds in all arenas of our material and immaterial realities (p. 32)!"

Read the numerous Scriptures listed from Pages 26-33.

a. What is the singularizing theme of the spirit/posture of the Church prior to the arrival of the Antichrist and the Second Coming of Jesus Christ?

b. How are cultural/global events and the increase in *lawlessness* directly connected to the *spirit* of the Church preceding the "*time of the end*"?

9. Describe how the following 3 attributes from 2 Timothy 3 & 4 *look* in the Western Church today:

HAVING THE *FORM* OF GODLINESS, BUT DENYING ITS POWER	ALWAYS LEARNING, *NEVER* ABLE TO ARRIVE AT THE *TRUTH*	PEOPLE WILL NOT ENDURE SOUND TEACHING

10. **Page 34 states,** "Good Shepherds prepare their people for suffering and endurance in a way that the *truth* and *hope* planted in them will spring up under the rushing waters of persecution. This is the basis of Psalm 1 and Jeremiah 17 (see also Ps 112). If we sow according to the Spirit, we will most certainly reap a harvest of power, boldness, hope, and steadfast love. However, if what is sown (by Hireling-Shepherds) is according to the flesh, we will most certainly reap fear, anxiety, discouragement, *cowardice*, and hopelessness."

Read: John 10:1-21, John 15:10-14, 2 Peter 2:1-3, 1 Timothy 4:1-2, 2 Peter 3:1-4, Acts 4:29-31, Philippians 1:20-30, Matthew 10:24-39, Jeremiah 17:5-8, Hebrews 10:32-39, 1 John 2:3-6

How do you distinguish a "Good Shepherd" from a "hireling"?

11. <u>Read:</u> 1 John 4:1, 2 Corinthians 13:5-8, Galatians 6:3-10, Revelation 2:1-7, 1 John 2:3-6, 15-17, James 3:13-16, James 4:1-10, Ephesians 5:3-20, Luke 21:34-36, 1 John 1:9, Colossians 2:13-15, Psalm 103:1-5

After reading Chapter 1 and *assessing the battlefield*, what are some *Critical Vulnerabilities* in your life, understanding/perceptions, home, or Church Body that must be "squared-away" in order to stand confidently and with great joy on the battlefield? Where have compromises been made?

1. _____

2. _____

3. _____

4. _____

5. _____

12. Offer some *biblically-based* solutions to standing anew as *literal* Warriors in a *literal* War. Describe the *tactical advantage* that these solutions provide in your *war efforts* in this generation:

BIBLICAL SOLUTIONS				
TACTICAL ADVANTAGE				

WARRIOR CLASS TACTICS AND STRATEGIES

1. *Acknowledge* the War; *study* the battle plan, the Word of the Lord.

2. *Conduct* your "Capabilities Assessment" with sincerity; it *must* be fluid and continuous.

3. *Assess* your Critical Vulnerabilities and the Critical Vulnerabilities of the Church with integrity.

4. *Be* the Body, the Warrior Class, to one another and in authentic love, aid in assessing the vulnerabilities and ability to stand in the day of battle.

5. *Repent* of any presumptions, negligence, apathy, or willful ignorance.

6. *Grow* in knowledge and depth of insight of the Kingdom of God *so that* you can begin to *rightly* discern.

7. *Understand* that you have been written into *The War*, and it *requires* your uncompromising devotion.

8. *Come out from* among the compromised and the complacent and be set apart.

9. *Refuse* to reduce the King of Glory, the Word of the Lord, or the power of the Holy Spirit.

10. *Reject* the spirit of the Age and walk in the Truth.

11. *Renew* your identity as a Warrior within the ranks of the Coming Conquering King, Jesus Christ, Who has a strategic, powerful, and blessed role for you to play.

12. *Rejoice* in the Lord and in the wonders of the *Good News*!

 # Battle Plan

OMEGA DYNAMICS FOR ADVANCING ON THE BATTLEFIELD	MY WARRIOR IDENTITY IN CHRIST JESUS

MY WEAPONS [VERSES] TO MEMORIZE:

HOW I WILL TAKE THE FIGHT TO THE ENEMY	MY BATTLEFIELD PRAYER

NOTES

SESSION 2

The Mission

It is time for the Body of Christ to take up our Commander's Intent and rightly accomplish the Mission charged to us. We must put to death the emotionally-patronizing idea of "love well" and "love wins" and enter into rightly loving the Lord and our neighbors. We must make war out of the same love from which our Warrior King has and is! Only by sacrificially loving the Lord our God because He first loved us (1 John 4:19) can we become Special-Purposed Warriors for the Kingdom who boldly take a stand....

The Warrior-Remnant must know who we are in Christ in order to be equipped to stand in and through the very difficult Missions ahead. Bold, courageous, unashamed, and poured-out: these are the attributes of the Lord's Warriors, emblazoned on the "dog tags" of our hearts. May the world around us be astonished and take note that we are on Mission in the Name and power of Christ Jesus (Acts 4:13). May we count the cost in its totality and know the precious worth of our surrendered lives. And as we steadfastly look at the One standing in front of us, our Perfect Operator, as well as to the right and left at those standing shoulder-to-shoulder within our ranks, we can endure to the end out of an overflowing deep, rich, Authentic Love!

Stand, People of God, and *persevere* in your Mission! Be strong and take heart and persevere in your Mission! (*O.D.*, p. 65-67)

1. **Page 40 states**, "Like in any military operation, it is paramount that the Warrior Saints of the Lord have a deep understanding of our Mission before stepping-off into the fray. From it flow all the necessary strategies, equipping, and stamina to see the arduous conflict through to overwhelming victory." This statement has powerful ramifications for the Redeemed of the Lord. Therefore, the task and purpose of this Chapter is to elucidate the *right* Mission Statement and the *right* Mission Set in order to equip the People of God with the courage, tenacity, humility, and love to *STAND* in this ever-darkening world.

In a single sentence, write a Mission Statement for the Redeemed of the Lord:

OUR MISSION IS: _____

_____

_____

2. **In your own words, describe how we, the Church, the Body of Christ, are the Commander's *Main Effort* in this multidimensional combat zone (p. 42):**

3. **"The reason the Son of God appeared was to destroy the works of the devil" (1 John 3:8b): How does this verse compare to your understanding/paradigm as to why Christ came and dwelt with men?**

4. **Read:** Revelation 17:14, Revelation 19:11-16, 1 Corinthians 15:24-28, Ephesians 1:17-23, Colossians 1:9-19, Colossians 2:9, 13-15, Hebrews 2:14-17, Acts 10:38, Matthew 16:18, Luke 12:49-51, Acts 26:15-18, Ephesians 6:10-12, 1 John 5:18-20, 1 John 3:4-10

a. **How do the above Scriptures challenge/differ from the reduced *version* of the Gospel often presented in church today?**

b. How does this challenge your understanding of Christ's Mission?

c. How does it invigorate and edify your understanding of Christ's Mission?

5. **In your own words, describe how dutifully conducting our Mission ultimately satisfies the Mission of Christ Jesus *and* the Mission of God the Father (p. 45):**

6. **"Jesus declared that the world will know we are Christians by our love.** And yet, the Church's very genetic coding -what 'love' is and what it is not- has been 'tampered' with by the 'Luciferian Whitecoats' in high places. Sadly, today's Church, and the fruit it yields, have become representative of a 'genetically modified organism' (GMO) (*p. 48*)."

How has the culture *defined* what "*Love*" is?

Read: James 3:14-16, 2 Peter 2:1-3, Romans 1:28-32, 1 Corinthians 5:3-12, Ephesians 5:3-14, Jeremiah 8:8-12, Jeremiah 23:10-18, Isaiah 5:18-23, Ezekiel 34:1-6, Hosea 4:5-9, Amos 5:21-24, Malachi 3:13-15

How has the Church _distorted_ what "_Love_" is and surrendered to the _World's_ definition?

7. Contrast the actions of *GMO Love* with the actions manifested by those who possess *Authentic Love*:

GMO LOVE	*AUTHENTIC* LOVE

8. **The single most significant characteristic of the Last Church Age is Its** *faulty* **self-perception** (Rev 3:15-19, 2 Cor 11:4); it is what clears the way for the Antichrist and his "Total War" against all of humanity (2 Thess 2:3).

Review the scriptures on Pages 49-51:

a. **What are some of the root causes for the Church's increasingly** *delusional* **perception of Itself?**

b. **The word** *"MANY"* **is used extensively to describe those who are** *claimants* **of Christianity but in** actuality give heed to cultural conformity as well as "seducing spirits" in the Last Church Age.

   [**Reference:** Matthew 24:4-14, Matthew 7:13-14, 21-23, Revelation 12:9, 1 John 4:1, Matthew 15:8-9, 1 Timothy 4:1-2, 2 Peter 2:1-3, etc.]

Examine yourself and your immediate Church Body: Is there anywhere you have conformed to the *"MANY"*? **If so, what** *sacrifices* **need to be made in a demonstration of** *Authentic Love* **for the Lord and the lost and hurting world around you?**

9. **Read:** Exodus 15:3, Isaiah 43:13, Joel 2:11, Luke 12:49-53, Jeremiah 20:11, Psalm 45:2-8, Revelation 19:11-16, Zephaniah 3:17, Psalm 24:8, Colossians 2:15, Revelation 17:14, 1 Corinthians 15:24-26

Why do most Christians reject (or dismiss) Jesus as a Warrior? Why do they compartmentalize/ separate the God of the Old Testament from the God of the New Testament? How does removing the attribute of Christ as a Warrior change our posture, perspective, and conduct in this life?

10. Review Pages 54-60: List several examples of how Christ Jesus demonstrated *Authentic Love* in fighting, warring, sacrificing and conquering! How is His Warrior-Spirit displayed in the war against sin, deception, lawlessness, wickedness, and the fight for truth, freedom, protection of the weak, etc.?

1. _____

2. _____

3. _____

4. _____

5. _____

11. Review Pages 60-63, the process of *"Selection"* for those who seek to become an *"Operator"* (Special Forces):

Describe how you *HAVE / HAVE NOT* fully counted the cost (Luke 14:25-33) of abiding in the True and Better Warrior Culture of the Lord as a "Solider of Christ". Would you give up your security, personal validation, relationships, comfort, job, finances, ambitions and aspirations, retirement, health, fears, your "kingdom", your very life, the life of your spouse, and most difficult of all, the lives of your children in steadfast devotion to the Mission of Christ *"so that others may live"*?

12. Those of the Warrior Class have counted the cost, but equally *know* the Commander they serve and the commendation that awaits.

<u>Read:</u> James 1:2-4, Romans 5:3-5, 1 Peter 4:12-19, Romans 8:18-21, Habakkuk 3:17-19, Matthew 5:10-12, 1 Peter 5:8-10, 2 Corinthians 4:13-18, 2 Timothy 3:12-17, 1 Peter 1:3-8, Revelation 2:10-11, Revelation 12:11

a. **What is your posture/emotion at the thought of it being *costly* to follow Christ [fearful, resentful, anxious, opposing, negotiating, withholding, rebutting, defiant, broken, etc. -or- steadfast, bold, hopeful, eager, willing, entrusted, etc.]?**

b. **Given the Scriptures above, what *should* our posture be and *why* can we be joyful, having "fully counted the cost"?**

c. **List the tangible, eternal rewards to those who "love not their lives unto death", who overcome, and who persevere:**

13. If you were to stand before our Commander-in-Chief and the Captain of our Salvation *this very day*, how would your Commendation Citation read (p. 64-65)?

FOR MERITORIOUS SERVICE TO THE KINGDOM OF HEAVEN unto the GLORY OF THE FATHER AND OF THE SON

PRESENTED TO MY FAITHFUL SERVANT AND CHILD THIS DAY, _____ OF _____:

GIVEN UNDER MY HAND, COMMANDER AND CHIEF OF THE HEAVEN'S ARMIES, ABBA-FATHER, FROM EVERLASTING TO EVERLASTING

14. Warriors are not weak, they are not passive, idle, indifferent, or cowardly; warriors fight to the death because warriors love hard! Christ Jesus is our True and Better Example of a Warrior.

a. *"Love will _____ _____ itself in the*

degree to which it is _____ to _____

toward the _____ of its love" is the maxim of Chapter 2.

b. For what are you willing to sacrifice?

c. For what will you physically and spiritually fight and make war (1 Tim 5:8)?

d. For what will you lay down your life?

15. After having read all of Chapter 2, describe how the Warrior-Spirit is at the foundation of our Mission to "*love* the Lord our God" and "*love* our neighbors":

WARRIOR CLASS TACTICS AND STRATEGIES

1. <u>*Know*</u> your Mission-Set and the Mission of your *Heavenly Leadership*.

2. <u>**Redeem**</u> what it is to *love*, and carry out your Mission anew in *Authentic Love*.

3. <u>**Take hold**</u> of Christ Jesus for Who He is: A *good*, *mighty*, Warrior-King.

4. <u>**Study**</u> the Word of the Lord and *be not* deceived.

5. <u>**Fix**</u> your eyes on the True and Better Operator, Christ Jesus.

6. <u>**Count**</u> the cost and get in the fight.

7. <u>**Make**</u> war against wickedness and all Enemies *foreign* (eternally) and *domestic* (internally).

8. <u>**Defend**</u> the oppressed, the captive, and the innocent out from a pure Warrior-Spirit.

9. <u>**Advance**</u> the Mission of the Lord forward in *Authentic Love* with the intensity of a warfighter.

10. <u>**Be**</u> *bold* and *courageous* in the days ahead through your identity in Christ Jesus.

11. <u>**Rejoice**</u> and *persevere* for the joy and *commendation* that is set before you as the Lord's Warrior Redeemed.

 # Battle Plan

OMEGA DYNAMICS FOR ADVANCING ON THE BATTLEFIELD	MY WARRIOR IDENTITY IN CHRIST JESUS

MY WEAPONS [VERSES] TO MEMORIZE:

HOW I WILL TAKE THE FIGHT TO THE ENEMY	MY BATTLEFIELD PRAYER

NOTES

_____

_____

_____

_____

_____

_____

_____

_____

_____

_____

_____

_____

_____

_____

SESSION 3

Identifying The Battlespace

In the midst of the cosmic war laid out from Genesis to Revelation, in the midst of the cosmic rescue plan of redemption through Jesus Christ laid out from Genesis to Revelation, YHWH forcefully declares there can be no neutrality, no apathetic involvement, and no obscurity of the battlefield in this Campaign. The nature of our "Total War" assures it! There is not, nor could there be, even one person in the whole of humanity since Adam in the Garden, who is able to claim the distinction of being a noncombatant. Every living thing and every aspect of created order is betrothed to this war. Therefore, due to the high-stakes reality of this conflict our Battlespace must be rightly divided (O.D., p. 73).

It is crucial for us, the Redeemed of the Lord, to remove any obscurity from our Battlespace! Any ambiguity, infiltrators, saboteurs, dissenters, or cowards within our ranks will garner devastating consequences in this coming Fight of the Ages. The Warrior Class must rightly discern and rightly divide the extremity of the Guerilla War and its belligerents. To be dismissive or complacent in any degree is to become a casualty of war. Know definitively in Whose battle formation you stand! Know definitively under Whose Banner you march! Be strong in the Lord and in His mighty power and arise to see the deliverance of the Lord!

The Warrior Class of the Most High must utterly repudiate the concept of engaging in Conventional Spiritual Warfare and employing Conventional tactics! Our war is Guerilla Warfare through and through; it always has been and always will be! With Sword in hand, we must renew our minds in an understanding of friend-from-foe and rightly discern the Battlespace about us (O. D., p. 96-97).

1. **Page 72**: When you do not understand your _____, when battle lines are _____, and friend-from-foe is difficult to distinguish, _____ and _____ reign supreme. There will be grievous _____.

2. "In the midst of the cosmic war laid out from Genesis to Revelation, in the midst of the cosmic rescue plan of redemption through Jesus Christ laid out from Genesis to Revelation," what 3 things does the Lord declare _cannot_ exist on the battlefield of His Campaign?

    1. _____

    2. _____

    3. _____

3. **Page 74 of _Omega Dynamics_ states:**

"Love wins" is the anthem of today's Church where too many feel that to befriend the culture is to become more effective for the Kingdom; to fellowship and acquiesce with the world is to make the gospel (no matter how compromised) acceptable to the masses. The marching orders sent out through the Laodicean congregations of today are: embrace, befriend, blur, whitewash, and compromise in the name of "love", tolerance, and relevance! And this, like any war-torn ground whose Battlespace is ambiguous (to which I can personally attest), has led to a great deal of chaos, confusion, and fratricide.

Read: Jeremiah 6:10, Jeremiah 2:19, Psalm 78:32-37, Proverbs 1:20-33, 2 Peter 2:1-3, Hosea 4:6-9, 2 Timothy 4:3-4, 2 Timothy 3:1-5, Jeremiah 8:8, 12, John 6:60-66, Matthew 13:10-15, Luke 14:25-35, Isaiah 30:8-13

Why do _many_ Christians assume a posture of denial or "neutrality" toward the war that rages around them? Why do you think many of those in positions of authority in the Christian Church choose not to equip the people to _rightly_ divide the world around them?

4. List some of the consequences in assuming "neutrality" in the war against sin and wickedness in your own life (your home, family/children, communion with the Lord, etc.), the Church, and the Nation:

EFFECTS OF THE SWITZERLAND TRESPASS

PERSONAL	CHURCH	NATION

5. Look at the list of "*Divisions*" on Page 78:

a. Why does the Lord Almighty make such distinct divisions about every facet of our being? How are we benefactors of His "divisions"?

b. How does the lost and dying world around benefit from the Warrior Redeemed making distinct, _right_ divisions amid the throes of combat?

6. **Page 79 states,** "A _war of attrition_ is taking place where the weak and weary saints, ill-equipped and ill-trained for the afflictions of war, are broken and battered because of the equally ill-defined Battlespace. Rather than being strengthened and outfitted with the Sword of the Spirit (The Word) and a deeply rooted identity in Christ Jesus, they are being sent into combat wearing tighty-whities (underwear) while wildly swinging their Smartphone in the air with a daily-devotion quip on its screen (p.79-80)."

How has the Church's failing to _rightly_ divide [unwillingness to make definitive distinctions between righteousness/unrighteousness or Eternal Truths/falsehoods] propagated a _war of attrition_ within the Body of Christ (Ezekiel 13)? How is it manifesting through the lawlessness and perversion in the world around us (p. 79-81)?

7. **Page 81 of _Omega Dynamics_ posits:** How then, do we ensure that we honorably and steadfastly hold the lines within our Battlespace? How do we repel infiltration into our camps and breaks in our ranks? How do we as Warriors of the Most High distinguish friend from foe, divide correctly, and bring about clarity amid the fog-of-war?

Read: John 1:1-5, Hebrews 4:12-13, Hebrews 5:11-14, Philippians 1:9-11, 1 Corinthians 2:6-16, 2 Timothy 2:15, 1 John 2:4-6, 2 Kings 22:18-19, Psalm 91:14-16, Malachi 3:16-4:3, 2 Corinthians 10:3-6

Detail how the Word (both Christ Jesus and the Sword) fully answers the questions above (_p. 81-85_):

8. a. An Insurgency, by definition, is: _____

_____.

b. <u>Read</u> the following verses and describe the extent of the Cosmic Insurgency: Jude 1:3-19, 2 Peter 2:4-22, Isaiah 14:3-21, Ezekiel 28:1-19, Psalm 2:1-3, Romans 3:10-12, James 4:4, Romans 1:18-32.

9. "As the operations of the Enemy Insurrectionists advance, we Warriors of the Lord must unswervingly be evaluating their ability to DRAW-D while also evaluating our ability to DRAW-D. Our ability to 'adapt and overcome' (a Marine Corps maxim) against all the affronts of the Adversary depends upon it. Just as the battlefield is dynamic and requires well-ingrained adaptability, so too does our 'fight against the rulers, against the authorities, against the cosmic powers over this present darkness, against the spiritual forces of evil in the heavenly places' (Eph 6:12) (p.87)."

a. Look at the acronym on Pages 86-87: Give an example of how Rebel Insurgents are currently using **DRAW-D** tactics in the Church and in our Culture:

	CHURCH	CULTURE
D		
R		
A		
W		
D		

b. **Thoroughly assess your ability to DRAW-D both spiritually and physically** [**Note:** If you are made aware of any vulnerabilities, identify and seek to strengthen them.]:

	SPIRITUALLY	PHYSICALLY
D		
R		
A		
W		
D		
MY VULNERABILITIES:		

10. The Warrior Class must _know_ and _understand_ Guerilla Warfare (p.86-92):

"Insurgents utilize extremely insurrectionary and asymmetric methods for achieving their desired End State. Their tactics are varied and lethal; they are often subtle yet full-scale and wide ranging. An insurgency does not abide by any fleeting notion of Rules of Engagement, Geneva Convention mandates, or civility. Anything and everything is fair game for harassment, disruption, sabotage, corruption, assassination and total annihilation (_p. 88_)."

a. **List and briefly describe each of the Tactics and Techniques of Rebel Insurgents (p. 89-92):**

1. _____ _____ and _____:

2. _____:

3. _____:

4. _____:

5. _____:

b. <u>**Thoughtfully analyze:**</u> Where have you and/or your immediate Church Body been assaulted by these *Guerilla Warfare* tactics?

c. Give 3 *Offensive Actions* you can take to strike a blow against the Insurgency:

1. _____

2. _____

3. _____

11. Describe some of the Enemy's *Scorched Earth Policy* (*p. 92-95*) already being seen in the world around you. List some of the aspects of this *Scorched Earth Policy* that will unfold in *Last Days*:

IS HAPPENING	*WILL* HAPPEN

12. "For every _____ there is a _____ and

well-coordinated _____ _____!

13. Write a prayer of *confession* and *repentance* for any area where you have allowed your Battlespace to become obscured, chaotic, or confused (Josh 24:14-15); where you have not *rightly* divided. End with a prayer of thanksgiving for the testimony of Jesus Christ, the Gospel of our Warrior King and the far-superior *Ranks* He has enlisted you into:

WARRIOR CLASS TACTICS AND STRATEGIES

1. <u>Read</u> Matthew 6:19-24, 2 Timothy 2:3-6, 1 Kings 18:21, Joshua 24:14-15, 2 Chronicles 16:9a, Revelation 3:15 and *make a choice*.

2. <u>Repent</u>, where you have been complacent!

3. <u>Repent</u>, where you have been complacent!

4. <u>Repent</u>, where you have been complacent!

5. <u>Close Ranks</u> (shore up your battle lines) by *rightly* dividing all things.

6. <u>Train</u> diligently as a Warrior of the Most High with *the Sword* (the Word) and *your Sword* (Christ Jesus).

7. <u>Stop</u> fighting with Conventional Tactics and start fighting a Counter Insurgency.

8. <u>Be Vigilant</u> for the tactics and techniques of Guerilla Warfare.

9. <u>Assess</u> your ability to *DRAW-D* continually; *adapt and overcome* through Christ Jesus.

10. <u>Praise</u> the Lord for His amazing grace that was and is lavished on us through Christ Jesus; He Who bore up under the full onslaught of the concentrated efforts of all the *Insurgent Rebels* and yet did not falter! *Worship* Christ Jesus, our Perfect Example in the face of battle and our Perfect Substitute when we succumb to it! Be comforted, strengthened, and reinvigorated by the breadth and depth of the *Good News* of our overwhelming victory on the field of battle!

Battle Plan

OMEGA DYNAMICS FOR ADVANCING ON THE BATTLEFIELD	MY WARRIOR IDENTITY IN CHRIST JESUS

MY WEAPONS [VERSES] TO MEMORIZE:

HOW I WILL TAKE THE FIGHT TO THE ENEMY	MY BATTLEFIELD PRAYER

NOTES

SESSION 4

Line of Departure: Purify Your Camp

Like those in Jerusalem under the leadership of Nehemiah, Warriors of God are to begin repairing the wall in front of our own houses first! Section by section and family by family we can rebuild our defenses and repel the attacks of the Enemy. Like those in Jerusalem, we are to work with one hand and maintain a sword in the other! Always vigilant, we must sleep with our clothes on until the disrepair of the "City that bears His name" is restored! Perhaps, rather than being pseudo-warriors for any social issue-du jour, we should be Kingdom Warriors who answer the Battle Cry of the Redeemed: "Remember the Lord, who is great and awesome, and fight for your families, your sons and your daughters, your wives and your homes" (Neh 4:14) (O.D., p. 113-114)!

Experience Revival in your heart as you live in a way to confidently proclaim, "But He knows the way that I take; when He has tested me, I will come forth as gold. My feet have closely followed His steps; I have kept to His way without turning aside. I have not departed from the commands of His lips; I have treasured the words of His mouth more than my daily bread" (Job 23:10-12) (O.D., p. 115).

There is a congruency regarding the clarion call of the Lord toward His people all throughout scripture: REPENT! The battle for the hearts and minds of men is such that only unmitigated allegiance to the commands and decrees of the Lord (His Word) will ensure our ability to stand among the Warrior Class. As with any high-stakes operation in life, any compromises- any chinks in your armor- will be exposed when the first rounds of the Enemy are fired down-range. We must not imperil the wondrous Mission, equipping, and overwhelming victory bestowed upon us which occurs when we fail to purify our camps.

It is time for men of God to *repent* of their treasonous leanings and arise! It is time for the women of God to *repent* of their torn allegiances and arise! It is time for the Church to *repent* of Its open sedition towards God Almighty and arise! Because of this we have been assured, "You cannot stand before your enemies until you take the devoted things (all that is to be surrendered to the Lord) from among you"!

Consider Chapter 4 carefully; there you will see 2 distinctions: the *conscripts* from the *Warriors* and the *causalities* from the *Conquerors*.

1. **Page 99 states,** "The Lord fully knows and completely understands the nature of war. He knows that the Adversary His people are going to encounter is so formidable, so tactically proficient, and has such great resources that only those whose hearts and minds are fully devoted to trusting in Him will win the day. Any contaminants to our singleness of mind make us liable to becoming a casualty. The Warriors of the Most High are to take heed."

   a. **After reading Joshua 7:3-15, identify several *devoted things* that have been *hidden* among the Church's *belongings*, making It turn Its back before Its enemies. In other words, why has the Western [American] Church been defeated on almost every social, cultural, political, and even spiritual battlefront for the past 80 years (prayer, legislated abortion, legislated perversion, freedom of speech, 501(c)(3) restraints, media influence, social engineering, sound doctrinal teaching, etc.)?**

   b. **The Enemy** _____ **with** _____

      as those with _____, _____

      loyalties lie wounded and maimed in the street as ineffectual _____

      in the war they do not _____! (Page 101)

   c. **Martin Niemöller (1892–1984),** a prominent Lutheran pastor in Germany during The Holocaust, made the following statement:

   First they came for the socialists, and I did not speak out—because I was not a socialist.

   Then they came for the trade unionists, and I did not speak out— because I was not a trade unionist.

   Then they came for the Jews, and I did not speak out—because I was not a Jew.

   Then they came for me—and there was no one left to speak for me.

What is the role of the Warrior Redeemed in the days ahead? Given the *velocity* and *intensity* of anti-Christian rhetoric, what do you perceive is in the near future for uncompromising Believers in Christ Jesus and His Eternal Word? Have you counted the cost of standing for truth and righteousness?

4. **Page 101 states**, "Sin encumbers, hinders, and acts as an infiltrating breach by the Enemy to impede the constant supply of resources from Heaven to the boots on the ground. This is why the Warrior Class is to 'hate the very clothing stained by sin' (Jude 1:23); it makes you a 'soft target' on the field of battle. It makes you unable to stand and vulnerable to great ruination."

a. This takes transparency and humility, but by it we exalt the power of the Gospel; and by it we make ourselves ready to advance on the battlefield!

Where have you experienced *demoralization*, had your nose "*bloodied*", or been outright *defeated* by Insurgent Forces because of the *chinks in your armor*? What acts of *treason, mutiny, or sedition* could be charged against you? What are the *devoted things* you have hidden (or are unwilling to surrender) that have made you "*liable*" *for destruction*?

BEEN BLOODIED	BEEN TREASONOUS	HIDDEN AWAY

b. What is the *Good News* of the "greatest act of *injustice* in the history of the world" (p. 102-103)?

5. Through an unceasing cycle of _____, _____, _____, _____, _____, _____, and _____ to God's commands (His Word) we increasingly become a _____ _____ _____ weapon in the hand of our Warrior King, Jesus, arresting the rebel within as well as those Rebels without (p. 103).

6. Page 103 states, "Remember, we cannot assume that simply because we bear the name of 'Christian' our prayers are powerful and effectual, or that the Enemy trembles in our presence."

Do you agree with the statement that "there are two kinds of Christians (p. 105)"? If so, what are some distinctions?

7. <u>Page 105</u>: The _____ _____ of the Church toward _____ has caused us to be the "_____" of the Heaven's Armies. We have conformed to the world instead of _____ that it _____ to us!

8. Page 108 states, "He [God Almighty] gave command to His People to 'come out' and 'touch no unclean thing' knowing that the violence of the War necessitates an unhindered attunement to His Spirit. He did this also knowing fully the treasonous leanings of our hearts to the enticements of the Enemy's seductions. Any deviation from unconditional surrender to God jeopardizes everything when the bullets start flying."

<u>Read:</u> 1 John 3:1-10, 1 John 5:1-5, 1 Corinthians 3:10-17, 2 Timothy 2:4-7, 20-22, Ephesians 5:1-17, Luke 21:34-36, Luke 12:42-49, Hebrews 10:26-36, 2 Corinthians 5:6-10, 2 Corinthians 7:1, 1 John 1:5-10, 1 John 2:1-6, 28-29

a. How are we to cultivate a *surrendered, loyal* Warrior Spirit that advances confidently on in *combat?*

b. <u>Read</u>: Exodus 33:18-19, Matthew 10:28, Hebrews 10:30-31, 1 John 4:7-19

What must our 3 *core beliefs* be about God in order to be wholly devoted to Him and to the fight?

    1. He is _____

    2. He is _____

    3. He is _____

9. Read the "consequences" of not coming out from among 'unholy men' (John Wesley, 1872) written on Pages 108-110:

List 5 *effects* (that stuck out to you personally) that result when Christians have a *compromised allegiance* with the world around them:

    1. _____

    2. _____

    3. _____

    4. _____

    5. _____

10. <u>Page 110</u>: It is one of the greatest displays of the grace of God when He _____

_____ anything that is a _____ to setting our _____

fully on Him.

11. "Praise be to God for our immovable Hope that the blood of Christ speaks a better word than the blood of Abel (Heb 12:24)! It has the power to cleanse and restore our fighting capabilities where we have allowed them to be compromised (p. 112)."

<u>**Read**</u>: Isaiah 1:16-20, James 4:8-10, Psalm 51:1-12, Psalm 103:1-5, 10-14, Ephesians 2:4-10, Colossian 2:6-15, 1 John 4:13-19

Write a personal psalm of worship to God for His grace, mercy, and loving-kindness in restoring a *right* Warrior-Spirit in us through His Son, Jesus Christ:

12. Read Nehemiah 4:

Describe in your own words where _Godly_ Revival can be found: Where is it initiated? Who leads it? How is it advanced? What needs to be done to ensure its ability to endure? How can we measure its effectiveness?

[<u>**Reference:**</u> 2 Chronicle 7:13-14, Isaiah 66:2, Ezekiel 18:30-32, 2 Corinthians 7:8-11, James 4:4-10, Acts 2:38, Acts 3:17-20, 1 John 1:9, Revelation 2:5, 1 Peter 1:13-23, 1 Peter 2:9-12, Philippians 1:9-14, Hebrews 10:32-39, Job 5:17-18, Acts 28:31, Acts 4:29-35, Philippians 2:1-2, Philippians 1:27, Proverbs 28:1, Matthew 10:21-25, 2 Timothy 3:12-13, 1 Peter 4:1-2]

13. <u>Write</u>: Job 23:10-12 _____

_____

_____

_____

_____

14. **As we the Church prophetically "toe" the** *Line of Departure*, **can you personally declare the above verse with confidence; that your allegiance is unwavering and the** *devoted things* **are continually being surrendered?** ("Not that [you] have already obtained this or [are] already perfect, but [that you] press on to make it [your] own, because Christ Jesus has made [you] His own." **Philippians 3:12**)

YOU CAN ONLY CIRCLE ONE

YES- I seek to work-out my salvation with fear and trembling; I yearn to increasingly fix my eyes on Christ Jesus, the Author and Perfecter of my faith; my identity in the love of God displayed for me in Christ Jesus *compels* me to forsake all else and move in faith and boldness; I am weak, weary, and sometimes wayward, but HE IS NOT; I confess, I repent, and I stand confidently in the completed work of Christ; I desire to honor the Lord because He loves me and I love Him; I have fully counted the cost and still found the Lord to be good; I am a Warrior in the ranks of the Lord of Heaven's Armies and I will not be shaken!

NO- I still desire to befriend the world and am not yet ready/ willing to throw off everything for the Captain of my Salvation; my identity and validation are deeply rooted in myself, my works, my image, my fears, and my longings for acceptance; I struggle to find delight in the commands and decrees of the Lord, sometimes even finding them burdensome; I have counted the cost of being *all-in* and have found it to be too high; I have *devoted things* buried in my tent I don't feel like I can ever surrender; I don't really want to, or feel as though I am able to, fight for my family, home, Church Body, and righteousness of God; if I am honest, I don't fully trust that the Lord is good, I don't really *fear* Him, and I have a hard time believing His unrestrained love for me. -Lord, reveal yourself to me; reveal my error to me; restore my eyesight and give strength to my wayward heart. Lord, I want to serve honorably in your ranks…come to my aid and *help me*!

WARRIOR CLASS TACTICS AND STRATEGIES

1. <u>**Stand**</u> as the Warrior Redeemed of the Lord and get prepared to cross that *Line of Departure*.

2. <u>**Purify**</u> your camp *so that* you can charge into battle confident, fierce, and unhindered.

3. <u>**Choose**</u> your building materials wisely; you only get one shot at it.

4. <u>**Get**</u> *serious* about your allegiance for Christ real fast.

5. <u>**Kill**</u> the deeds of the flesh.

6. "<u>**Confess**</u> and <u>**repent**</u> and <u>**rejoice**</u>…then do it again and again until He returns, or you breathe your last."

7. <u>**Seek**</u> sincere, authentic Revival in your heart, mind, and home NOW!

8. <u>**Read**</u> 1 John 2:1-3 and praise the Lord!

9. <u>**Read**</u> 1 John 3:19-24 and praise the Lord!

10. <u>**Read**</u> 1 John 4:8-19 and praise the Lord!

11. <u>**Read**</u> 1 Peter 1:3-6 and praise the Lord!

12. <u>**Read**</u> Psalm 103 and praise the Lord!

13. <u>**Grit**</u> your teeth, *narrow* your eyes, and ***GET IN THE FIGHT!***

Battle Plan

OMEGA DYNAMICS FOR ADVANCING ON THE BATTLEFIELD	MY WARRIOR IDENTITY IN CHRIST JESUS

MY WEAPONS [VERSES] TO MEMORIZE:

HOW I WILL TAKE THE FIGHT TO THE ENEMY	MY BATTLEFIELD PRAYER

NOTES

SESSION 5

Courage Under Fire

The Warrior Saints of the Lord must grow and mature in our knowing of the Fear of the Lord and allow the floodwaters of courage to sweep over us in the heat of the battle. Preach the Good News of the Spirit of Power, Love, and Soundness of Mind which He has caused to dwell within us daily! Rebuke those perpetrators of "Stolen Fear" in the power of the Name of Jesus Christ and stand in the might of the Lord. Be jealous of His Fear as He is jealous for yours (O.D., p. 146).

1. **Page 117 states,** "Whether we realize it or not, almost every aspect of our daily reality can be reduced and attributed to fear. Although this is a strong assertion, if we can honestly evaluate ourselves (which is difficult, I know) we would capitulate to just how true this concept is."

Examine your life, relationships, thoughts, intentions, many of your actions, etc. Where can you discern the *truth* in the above statement on a personal level? Where has the Church and Church Leadership succumbed to fear? (**Examples:** I can't discipline my kids because they won't like me; I can't reduce my reality and focus on my family because I'll lose my sense of validation *and* money; I refuse to acknowledge the world around me because it makes me fearful; I can't be authentic with where I'm at because I won't look like a *"good"* Christian; I have to serve so people know I'm a dedicated Christian; I don't ever want to seem offensive or divisive; I [Pastor] have to tell the people what they want to hear or they will send me negative emails, stop coming to church, etc.):

2. <u>FINISH THE STATEMENT</u>: FEAR MISPLACED _____

_____ ;

FEAR RIGHTLY PLACED _____

_____

3. "Fear is a contagion (p. 118-121)." Give examples of the effects of *Fear of Man* versus *Fear of the Lord*:

FEAR OF MAN	FEAR OF THE LORD
1.	1.
2.	2.
3.	3.
4.	4.
5.	5.

4. **Page 122 states,** "Absolutely nothing in our natural reality will lay bare a person more thoroughly than what springs forth in the presence of overwhelming dread. This is true in the most minute of details of life (i.e. relationships, job choices, parenting styles, money habits, etc.) as well as in its mega-hardships (death, loss, betrayal, war, the supernatural, the hidden things in the world around us, etc.). The physiological and psychological effects of fear on the human body are profound."

Generally speaking, how do you respond to the stimulus of fear (synonymous with striving/stress/anxiety/worry/despair/distress)?

5. <u>**FINISH THE STATEMENT**</u>: THE OBJECT OF FEAR BECOMES, _____

_____, _____

_____ (p. 123)

6. **Fill in the _PERVERSE POSITIVE FEEDBACK LOOP_ affecting many Churches (p. 124):**

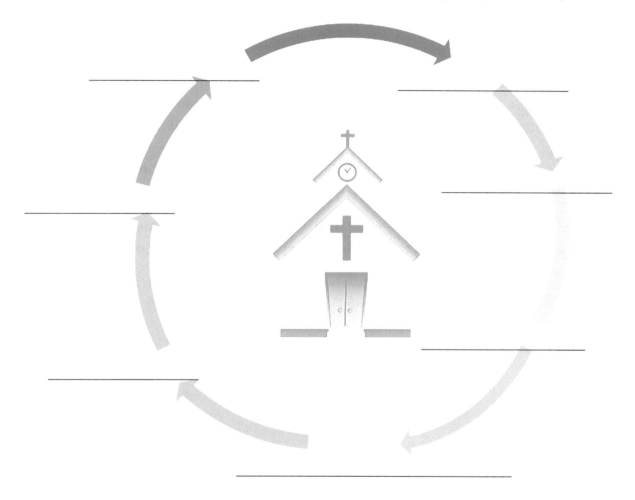

7. **"The failure to 'strive lawfully' will be this generation's undoing if not accompanied by sincere, undone repentance.** If we only aggrandize our own emotional well-being; if we champion being as innocent as doves without shrewdness; if we long to be acceptable to all men without being conscious of our acceptability before a Holy God; if we embrace the title "children of light" without taking up the follow-on command to 'expose the darkness'; if we are full of grace but offer no truth (which makes men free); if we are full of truth, but offer no grace (which we have been freely given); if we continue to proudly proclaim we are 'disciples' without the discipline (i.e. Disciple-en); if we shout aloud how much we love Him, yet do not follow His commands (1 John 2:3-6); and if we applaud the covering of Christ while rebuking the suffering that accompanies it, then we too have entered a de facto state of lawlessness and have thus become 'disqualified' (p. 127)."

In what ways have you *tipped-the-scales* in favor of one attribute/command of the Lord while neglecting other "less appealing" ones?

8. **The Warrior Class of the Most High must have a deep *knowing* of the Fear of the Lord** (Deut 5:29, Isa 8:11-13). "The Lord Most High possesses the fullness of understanding of Fear. It motivates, captivates, steers, spurs, and cautions. It engrosses all of us!... The Enemy, too, understands the power of fear. The Enemy understands the jealousy of God for your fear. The Enemy knows how it consumes, directs, distracts, motivates, and narrows your focus. This is why it is his number one tool; his strategic weapon of choice (p. 132)."

a. **Review the list of verses regarding the Fear of the Lord (p. 128-130): How is it strategically significant in our physical and spiritual fight that the Warrior Redeemed *rightly* fear the Lord?**

b. **What is the strategic significance and consequence of the Enemy hijacking your fear? How is the removing of the Fear of the Lord from our churches and pulpits a powerful tactic of the Enemy?**

9. Do you *believe* that exposing your fearfulness/anxiousness/insecurity is an act of *mercy* from the Lord? What <u>should</u> the exposure of your fearfulness cause you to do (p. 133-136)?

10. **Page 136 states**, "…where *Fear* has maintained a Command Post in your life and you have had the 'god of fear' placed above the God *to be* Feared, repent!"

a. **Where do you need to repent for allowing *misplaced* fear to maintain a stronghold in your life?**

b. **Why/how can we have a <u>*confident, secure, and joyous*</u> identity even in our fearful failings (Hint: p. 137)?**

11. <u>COMPLETE THE SENTENCES (p. 139-140):</u>

a. Fearlessness, _____ _____, magnifies the _____

and _____ _____ that *is* in Christ Jesus.

b. There is a direct correlation between _____ - _____

and the exaltation of what _____ _____ in Christ.

c. Our steadfast _____ and _____ during

the throes of combat makes the Rebel Insurgents _____.

d. This is why "_____ _____ _____" is never issued as

a _____ by the Lord, but rather as a direct _____!

12. Contrast those who remain under the *Shadow of Death* versus we Warriors who are *Children of Light* (p. 143):

DARKNESS/REBELS	LIGHT/RIGHTEOUS

13. <u>Complete this quote from Page 144:</u> In light of all this wonderful news, stand in the power of Christ that is in you and make much of the Lord you serve. In Him we are _____,

_____, _____, _____, _____,

_____, _____, _____,

_____, _____, _____,

_____, and _____ with a strength of mind that is

completely delivered, protected, secure, and sound! We are _____!

14. Why is it so crucial that the Warrior Class of the Lord understands that *Courage Exalts Christ* (p. 145)?

WARRIOR CLASS TACTICS AND STRATEGIES

1. <u>**Understand**</u> the powerful effects of Fear.

2. <u>**Realign**</u> any misplaced Fear.

3. <u>**Take hold**</u> of great courage for today, and whatever may lay ahead, by *first* succumbing to overwhelming *fear…the Fear of the Lord!*

4. <u>**Reject**</u> any "half-truthiness" being adopted by our church cultures and "strive lawfully" as you walk in the *right* Fear of the Lord.

5. <u>**Study**</u> the blessing and admonishments regarding the Fear the of Lord *so that* you can begin to walk in confident courage.

6. <u>**Fight**</u> for one another, for the Body, and for the Church against the Insurgents' strategic tactic to *steal away* our fear.

7. <u>**Turn**</u> toward the merciful, loving, and good Captain of our Salvation and allow the exposure of our misplaced fears to begin to shore-up and solidify our identity in Christ Jesus.

8. <u>**Fix**</u> your eyes on and magnify the True and Better Example of *Courage Under Fire*, Christ Jesus, and stand with all boldness.

9. <u>**Make**</u> darkness tremble and flee during the throes of battle by your steadfast identity as a Warrior of the Lord because of the confidence of Christ *in you*!

 # Battle Plan

OMEGA DYNAMICS FOR ADVANCING ON THE BATTLEFIELD	MY WARRIOR IDENTITY IN CHRIST JESUS

MY WEAPONS [VERSES] TO MEMORIZE:

HOW I WILL TAKE THE FIGHT TO THE ENEMY	MY BATTLEFIELD PRAYER

NOTES

SESSION 6

Baptism By Fire

Suffering upon sufferings and persecution upon persecutions are assured (Amos 5:18-20, Isaiah 24:17-18, 2 Timothy 3:12). However, we look to Christ Jesus who, "for the joy set before him endured the cross", and we too persevere for the joy that is set before us! Do not shrink back from entering Gethsemane. Do not shrink back from the preparation unto preferment. Allow the Lord to do whatever it takes to release the anointing oil upon you and through you for this generation. Allow the reduction to have its work so that He can build you up into His true and better identity as Steadfast Warriors in an imperishable Kingdom.

His desire is that you triumph in your Baptism by Fire with exceedingly great prowess. His desire is that you are able to carry His Baptism by Fire in order that you would go forth and "do exploits"! The harvest is plentiful, the workers are few, and the Enemy is ferocious; therefore, Make Ready for the final fire, and as the Warrior Class Saints, move in the knowing of the Lord!

So do not throw away your confidence; it will be richly rewarded. You need to persevere so that when you have done the will of God, you will receive what he has promised. For, "In just a little while, he who is coming will come and will not delay." And, "But my righteous one will live by faith. And I take no pleasure in the one who shrinks back." But we do not belong to those who shrink back and are destroyed, but to those who have faith and are saved.
Hebrews 10:35-39

"LOOK, I AM COMING SOON. MY REWARD IS WITH ME."

Rev. 22:11 (*O.D., p. 174-175*)

1. **In the Introduction to Chapter 6 we read,** "The *Day* has arrived where both the *mettle* and the *metal* of the Warrior Remnant of the Lord will be thoroughly tested."

a. "*Sand Table*" (role-play and work out the details) what your mental, emotional, spiritual, and even your physical response would be to a worst-case scenario (i.e. societal collapse, unimaginable persecution, refugee status, starvation, war, etc.) as well as to your personal worst-case scenario (great loss, obscurity, loneliness, etc.).

If your *Baptism by Fire* occurred this very day, how would your *mettle* (fortitude, bravery, resolve, steadfastness, soundness of mind) and your *metal* (strength, durability, confidence of the promises of the Lord) fare? What actions would you take physically, emotionally, and spiritually?

b. **After working out your "Sand Table": Where is your overall preparedness, confidence, and identity in Christ strong and well? What are some areas of your *mettle/metal* that need to be strengthened?**

2. COMPLETE THE SENTENCE: WARRIORS MUST _____ _____

   FOR THE _____ WE ARE _____ _____ IN!

3. **"To our detriment,** we often do not dare to embrace the reduction, the exceedingly great, costly, prolonged reduction, that occurs *prior* to being able to sustain the "Baptism by Fire" needed to honorably complete the Mission handed to us. There is always preparation, which occurs through refinement and sanctification, before the demonstration of the mighty hand of the Lord (p. 153)."

READ THE FOLLOWING VERSES: Write what our time of testing and reduction is _supposed_ to accomplish in us.

DESERT WARFARE TRAINING

NUMBERS 13:17-18	
JUDGES 3:1-4	
PROVERBS 17:3	
ISAIAH 1:25-27	
PSALM 66:8-12	
JAMES 1:2-4,12	
1 PETER 1:6-7	
JOB 23:10-12	
EXODUS 16:4	
DEUTERONOMY 8:2, 16	
HEBREWS 11:6	
1 PETER 4:1-2	
NUMBERS 13:17-18	

4. **Page 159 states,** "The desert wilderness is NOT intended to be a place of rebellion! It is the place where the Most High draws only those He loves so He can adequately equip us to execute the special purpose for which we have been foreknown; where our posture transforms from self-reliance and pride to meekness and humility. It is the place where He crushes the Egypt out of us; all the pagan, worldly, carnal, self-reliant, haughty, cowardly *garbage*! It is the place where He beats the Hell out of us! ...the hell in our minds, hearts, and souls that sets itself up against His Kingdom Objectives and *steals* from His glory."

What has been your response/posture to the times of being led into the wilderness, dry places; the times of testing, trial, waiting, and longings not yet realized? (<u>Reference</u>: Psalm 73:1-2, Proverbs 13:12, Proverbs 19:3, Psalm 78, Philippians 2:14-16, Numbers 14:1-4, 24-29, Exodus 17:2-7, 1 Corinthians 10:1-2)

5. **Review Pages 160-162. List at least 5 EXAMPLES of the blessings that arise from *Desert Warfare*:**

   1. _____

   2. _____

   3. _____

   4. _____

   5. _____

6. **COMPLETE THE SENTENCE FROM PAGE 165:**

   The _____ - _____ intention of all the thrashing, discipline, arduous "rucking", sleeplessness, hardship, and suffering (all the required physical endurance and mental fortitude) _____ _____ for what they have been at work _____: the achievement of _____ _____ on the day of battle!

7. **"YET ALL THIS WAS THE WAY TO HIS PERFERMENT":**

    a. **What was the purpose and outcome of all the *crushing*, *smelting*, and *reduction* that occurred in the life of Joseph? What was the purpose and outcome of this same *crushing* that occurred in Christ Jesus?**

    b. **What *has/is crushing* and *reduction* producing in your own life?**

    c. **Think about the difference between Judas Iscariot and Peter.** Both betrayed their friend and Savior, yet each chose to respond differently to what was exposed *in* them by their *fiery ordeal* (Judas choosing prideful self-preservation and Peter choosing humility unto preferment).

    In what ways have you sought to escape the *crucible* of being reduced for the sake of pride, comfort, or self-preservation? What is the effect of avoiding/abstaining from/quitting the process and purpose of *refinement* and *crushing*? [**Side Note**: Often overlooked forms of pride can be self-pity, guilt, shame, resentment, superficiality, defensiveness, the need of validation from others (fear of man), etc.]

8. Just as the anguish, suffering, and crushing experienced by our True and Better Warrior, Christ Jesus, was producing something, so too will that which is experienced by each of us. "We as Warriors of the Almighty must willingly allow the work that He has begun in each and every one of us to be completed. We must 'let steadfastness have its full effect, that [we] may be perfect and complete, lacking in nothing' (James 1:4). Not one ounce of our being undone for the sake of Christ will be wasted (p. 170)."

Read the verses on Pages 171-173. List 7 EFFECTS that *grueling training* (suffering/trial) produces in the heart of a Warrior:

EFFECT OF STEADFASTNESS IN TRAINING

1.	5.
2.	6.
3.	7.
4.	Do you consider suffering for the sake of Christ a joy and honor? YES / NO

9. <u>In intimate and intensive evaluation:</u> What do you need to solidify, shore-up, reinvigorate, or renew regarding your identity as a Redeemed Warrior of the Lord in order to receive your *Baptism* <u>by</u> *Fire* and *Baptism* <u>in</u> *Fire*? What confidence and assurance do we have in Christ to encourage a weary heart?

10. 1 PETER 5:6-11

_____

_____

_____

_____

_____

_____

_____

_____

_____

_____

_____

WARRIOR CLASS TACTICS AND STRATEGIES

1. **Read:** Habakkuk 2:3, Hebrews 10:32-39, Hebrews 12:1-4, 2 Corinthians 4:16-18.

2. **Test** yourself and to see if you would be able to withstand your *Baptism by Fire.*

3. **Do not test** and rebel against the Lord in the *Wilderness.*

4. **Pray** and ask the Lord to reveal to you the beauty of the Desert Wilderness.

5. **Pray** and ask the Lord to reveal to you how lovingly-merciful it is to be called into *Desert Warfare Training.*

6. **Repent** of where you have been rebellious, resentful, or *"shrinking back"* from the *Desert!*

7. **Train** for the fight you are *not yet in* physically, emotionally, and spiritually!

8. **Let** the *Training Program* of the Lord have its full effect in you *so that* you can stand among the Warrior Saints of the Most High.

9. **Seek** an increased *knowing* of the Lord in preparation for the *final fire* and the great *Last Days* harvest!

"...Listen to the voice of the Lord lovingly calling you into the wilderness where He can display His wondrous ways. Follow His beckoning to come out from Egypt and trust in His goodness. With renewed eyesight, look to the once desolate wasteland of the desert and see its uniquely stunning beauty.

Rest there. Quiet yourselves there. Be purged of Egypt and Babylon there as you begin to hear His voice anew. Receive His provisions there with gladness. Watch in amazement as He fights your Enemies in open terrain. Go, go and Tabernacle with Him there and learn from Him. Be amazed on the day of battle when all that was being worked deeply into your soul is revealed for its greatness (p. 174)."

 # Battle Plan

OMEGA DYNAMICS FOR ADVANCING ON THE BATTLEFIELD	MY WARRIOR IDENTITY IN CHRIST JESUS

MY WEAPONS [VERSES] TO MEMORIZE:

HOW I WILL TAKE THE FIGHT TO THE ENEMY	MY BATTLEFIELD PRAYER

NOTES

_____

_____

_____

_____

_____

_____

_____

_____

_____

_____

_____

_____

_____

SESSION 7

Make Ready!

Listen! Warriors of the Heaven's Armies, our command has gone out from the Most High, "Make Ready!" The trumpet has sounded a clear call by God's faithful Watchmen, "Condition 1"! Insurgent strongholds and offensive operations are reaching the culminating zenith. Like the coordinated surge of the enemy onslaught during the "Tet Offensive" of 1968 in Vietnam, the Insurgent Enemy of Creation has crawled out from the dense foliage of the jungles to wage war in open ground!

We are currently living in prophetic times unlike anything that has been since the Antediluvian Age of Noah (Genesis 6), and just shortly thereafter. Christ Jesus forewarned His followers of these exceedingly tumultuous Days when He proclaimed, "For then there will be great tribulation, such as has not been from the beginning of the world until now, no, and never will be. And if those days had not been cut short, no human being would be saved [there would be no flesh left alive]. But for the sake of the elect those days will be [shortened]" (Matt 24:21-22). We are in the midst of a convergent epoch, an advent which God, in the amazing mercy, laid out for us thousands of years ago in His Holy Scriptures. The Holy Spirit is now affirming these "things" to those with ears to hear. God's Word tells us all that will occur (... is occurring) so that we will not be caught unaware or deceived; so that our relationship in Christ Jesus will be solidified as our identity and hearts are strengthened unto overflowing in His loving faithfulness towards us. However, much of the Body of Christ has not been thoroughly equipped for what lies ahead. Still further, most who have "heard" and are aware, have not heeded the forewarnings in any measurable way. And so we sit, some aware, most not, exposed and vulnerable to attack. We sit poised for calamitous ruination within our camps! This should not be said of the Warrior Class of the Most High (O.D., p. 179-180)!

1. **Page 181 states**, "The *presumption* of dominance on the battle field, devoid of proper preparation and mindset, is the *assumption* of defeat. The presumption of 'superiority' while training and operating in 'inferiority' is an assurance of affliction. Those who fail to narrow their eyes and become sober-minded will fall on the field of battle. Those who ignored the charge to be hypervigilant, living and operating in "Condition 1", will experience great loss."

Read: Hosea 9:7-9, Luke 12:54-56, Luke 21:29-36, 2 Peter 3:1-10, Matthew 25:1-13, Revelation 1:1-3, Matthew 24:42-44, Revelation 16:13, Luke 12:35-49, 1 Thessalonians 5:1-8, 19-34, Mark 13:32-36, Revelation 19:10

Why do you think this current Church Age is the most *prophetically* and *intellectually* illiterate Church Age; why do most Western Christians deliberately "treat prophecies with contempt"? [**Hint:** Proverbs 1:20-33, Proverbs 2:22-26, Jeremiah 5:12-13, Isaiah 30:8-11, Hosea 4:6-9, 2 Timothy 4:1-5, Exodus 8:10-14]

2. **Read:** Jude 1:20-23, Romans 8:18-25, 2 Peter 3:10-13, Philippians 3:17-21, Ephesians 5:8-16, 1 Peter 1:3-9, 13-17, Hebrews 12:25-29, 2 Corinthians 5:1-11, Hebrews 11:13-16

"The Second Coming of Jesus Christ is the single greatest prophetic theme in Scripture (p. 183)."

Contrast the Lord's intent for the Church to focus their eyes on Christ's Return (positive: *eager anticipation, longing, looking, waiting,* etc.) <u>VERSUS</u> the consequences of the Church failing to do so (negative: *indifferent, deceived, powerless, earthly-minded,* etc.):

EAGER ANTICIPATION	INDIFFERENCE

3. Examine your paradigm/perspective of the image you hold of Christ Jesus (p. 184-187): Do you view Him more through the lens of *Messiah ben Joseph* or *Messiah ben David*? Do you tend to focus more on the Empty Cross (Christ's atonement for your sin) or do the eyes of your heart focus more on the Empty Tomb (Christ's power over life/death in you through the Holy Spirit)? Why do you *lean* more one way than the other?

[**Note:** There is no right or wrong answer; the great working and power of the Gospel is in *all and all*. This is merely an exercise to guide us to broaden our perspectives and enjoy coming into a more complete understanding of our Wonderful Warrior-King, Christ Jesus (Romans 6:1-18, 1 Peter 1:3-9).]

4. **Page 189-190 states,** "The Church has acquired an insatiable appetite for earthly affluence. It vehemently rejects the prophetic, especially as it relates to those things which are coming to pass prior to Christ's Return. Like the ostrich who buries its head in the sand while leaving the entirety of its body exposed, those who fill the seats of today's churches are ignorant of, or refuse to encounter, the reality surrounding them. The amassing of physical, emotional, and quasi-spiritual prosperity is the order of the day."

a. **Why do most Western Christians (those in the Pulpits and those in the Pews) dismiss Bible Prophecy and understanding of emerging events, trends, and threats? Why do many go so far as to discourage the Body/Church from giving attention to these topics?**

b. **In contrast, why do you think the Persecuted Church scattered throughout the world has an intimate focus on Bible Prophecy?** [**Reference:** Revelation 6:9-11, Revelation 20:4-6, 2 Peter 3:11-13, Romans 8:18-25, Isaiah 28:5-6, Psalm 149:6-9, 1 Corinthians 6:2-3, Psalm 37:28-29, Isaiah 30:18-19, Isaiah 51:4-5, Psalm 126:5-6]

5. PAGE 193: "We cannot be _____ - _____ and expect to fight this

fight without consequence! We will not survive '_____ _____ '

with those Luciferian Insurgents while we entertain the *world*! _____

equips us to strike quickly and accurately at the harassment of the Enemy Insurgents. It establishes

an unassailable _____ perimeter so that we do not succumb to

_____, acquiesce to our _____

_____, or get _____ off the battlefield by our Foe.

6. **Page 195 states,** "How we wear our Armor, and the discipline with which we maintain it, matters! It matters how we Hard-Target through prayer, confession, repentance, fasting, worship, reading of the Scriptures, fellowshipping with other brothers and sisters, and engaging the world around us! It matters how sound are our Situational Awareness and battlefield intelligence regarding Enemy tactics, techniques, and procedures in these anarchic days! Our very "posture" and daily, unwavering discipline determine the harassing fire and ambushes that are going to beset us! Enemy Insurgents from the pits of Hades are watching and discerning whom they can engage with the greatest chance of success. They are well versed in distinguishing the 'conscripts' from the Warriors. Get locked on, Church! You are in a war; put your head on a swivel, get squared-away, and get in the fight!"

a. **Describe the ways in which you are currently standing vigilant as a *"Hard Target"* against the Enemy's tactics and strategies in this generation: Where are you *"Hard Targeting"* your heart, home, church, and the glory of the Lord in your life? Where do you need to *harden* yourself, your family, and your Church Body?**

b. **What are some consequences of remaining a *"Soft Target"* on a personal level as well as on a Church-Body level on the field of battle?**

7. Often we become fixated on the _fruit_ of Evil (i.e. cultural perversion, emerging technologies, geopolitical strife, lukewarmness in the Church, etc.) rather than dealing with Its _roots_. Discuss what you personally see taking place as the _root cause_ for "_abounding iniquity_", and WHY (p. 196-197):

   -BE SPECIFIC

8. a. List 5 effects that being watchful, vigilant, and aware _should_ accomplish in a Warrior (p. 198):

   1. _____

   2. _____

   3. _____

   4. _____

   5. _____

   b. How would maintaining a _Hypervigilance_ for the Second Coming of Jesus Christ change your personal reality, focus/aspirations, and ministry?

9. <u>Note:</u> There are many in the Church who believe an attunement to Biblical Prophecy, "*unsanctioned/fringe*" information [*Extra-Biblical Teaching*], and the Second Coming of Jesus Christ are distracting, disruptive, or even detrimental to the simplicity and purity of the Gospel.

a. Is *Hypervigilance* compatible with love, joy, peace, patience, faithfulness, contentment, proclaiming the Kingdom of God, the *Great Commission*, etc. -WHY or WHY NOT?

b. In what ways *do* people <u>use</u> *Hypervigilance/Extra-Biblical Teaching* to the detriment of their hearers? In what ways *do* people <u>dismiss</u> *Hypervigilance/Extra-Biblical Teaching* to the detriment of their hearers?

WARRIOR CLASS TACTICS AND STRATEGIES

The Omega Dynamics for Chapter 7 are simple yet powerful: *GET LOCKED ON AND GET IN THE FIGHT!* It is your calling, election, and enlistment as a Redeemed Warrior of the Most High. Solidify the identity that is yours through Christ Jesus and His completed work, exemplified by both the *Empty Cross* and the *Empty Tomb*.

1. <u>Read:</u> Philippians 3:12b, Ephesians 5:16, 1 Thessalonians 5:5-8, 1 Peter 1:13-16, 1 Peter 4:7, and Luke 21:29-36.

2. <u>Live and act</u> in a way that you would be counted among *Gideon's 300*.

3. <u>Be found</u> among those who hear and keep the prophetic Word of the Lord.

4. <u>Walk</u> with Christ in this life as a *Hard Target*.

5. <u>Maintain</u> a sober mind and singleness of mind.

6. <u>Be</u> *Alert*, *Watchful*, and *Ready!*

7. <u>Grow</u> in your inward longings for a "better county-a heavenly one" (Heb 11:16).

8. <u>Hold out</u> the greatest truths and the greatest Hope, Christ Jesus, to this crooked and perverse generation.

9. <u>Trim</u> your wicks, maintain a store of the oil of the Holy Spirit, and be found watching for His Return.

10. <u>Serve</u> as ambassadors of the Righteousness of Christ.

11. <u>Honor</u> the Warrior Class to which you have been called.

12. *<u>Repent</u>* where you have been found to fall short, (1 John 1:9, James 4:7-10).

13. **MAKE READY, GO CONDITION 1!**

Battle Plan

OMEGA DYNAMICS FOR ADVANCING ON THE BATTLEFIELD	MY WARRIOR IDENTITY IN CHRIST JESUS

MY WEAPONS [VERSES] TO MEMORIZE:

HOW I WILL TAKE THE FIGHT TO THE ENEMY	MY BATTLEFIELD PRAYER

NOTES

SESSION 8

The Warrior Culture

Throughout history, warrior cultures have arisen from within various societies to create a distinctive caste. These warrior cultures are founded upon specific moral codes and a unique ethos which promote the group over the "person" and the Mission over the "individual". They are rooted in selfless sacrifice, honor, devotion to duty, dynamism, and a resolute inner strength to honor the greater good for which they fight (p. 202).

"Whosoever calls upon the name of the Lord shall be saved" (Rom 10:13) is a powerful, joyful, and eternal truth. So too is the truth that whosoever has been redeemed by the Blood of Jesus Christ has now been recruited to the True, Better, and Eternal Warrior Class! Although few Christians feel as though they are mighty warriors in the ranks of the Lion of Judah, the truth of the matter remains: YOU ARE! This, Beloved, is your identity! It is not founded upon anything you have achieved (lest anyone should boast) but upon the completed work of Christ Jesus and the newness of identity He lavishes upon His brethren!

This is why Page 238 boldly proclaims, "Now hear the Good News, 'Gideons' of the Most High. You who are anything but a Warrior. You who are feeble and infirm in spirit or body; who live in obscurity. You who are simpleminded and unlearned; who feel as though you are the 'least' within your reality; you who are grieved by your backsliding and apathy toward your King: God in His mercy, in the furtherance of His Kingdom Mission, and in exceeding great love, beckons you over and over again into His Warrior Culture! He does this without weariness or reproach because of His unfailing love and goodness. He is doing a new thing in this generation. The climax of this battle necessitates it! Take heart, be strong, and advance with extraordinary courage because you are in the ranks of The One Who 'calls those things that are not as if they were' (Rom. 4:17)!"

"Behold, the former things have come to pass, and new things I now declare; before they spring forth I tell you of them." **Isaiah 42:9**

We need to throw off the former things and allow the Good Word of the Lord to foster within us a new thing: our identities as Warriors for the Kingdom of God, through the power of the Gospel *already* at work *in* us!

As you grow in your understanding of a Warrior Culture (Chapter 8), begin to transform your perspective from that of a *helpless spectator* watching the scenes of war on the Nightly News, to that of a dynamic, active, and forcible Warrior for Truth and Love unto the Glory of God and the souls of men!

Remember: A Warrior will never be defined by status, disposition, health, age, competencies, intellect, and accomplishments, but by *spirit*…and that *spirit* is founded upon love, hope, trust, and obedience to the One Who is *Semper Fidelis* (*Always Faithful*)!

1. **Page 203 states:** "We must first understand the attributes of a Warrior Class so that we can arise and take our positions as the Warrior Class. As the days advance, may it be said of the Church of Jesus Christ that 'uncommon valor was a common virtue.' The charge has been issued: Arise, shine, for your light has come, and the glory of the Lord has risen upon you. For behold, darkness shall cover the earth, and thick darkness the peoples; but the Lord will arise upon you, and His glory will be seen upon you. And nations shall come to your light, and kings to the brightness of your rising (Isa 60:1-3)."

When you hear the word *Valor*, what kind of imagery does it evoke? Describe what living a Christian life of *Valor* would actually look like day-to-day (in your heart, thoughts, home, pursuits, churches, communities, etc.):

2. **In your own words list several differences that distinguish *Conscripts* from the *Warrior Class* (p. 204-207):**

CONSCRIPTS	WARRIORS
1.	1.
2.	2.
3.	3.
4.	4.
5.	5.

3. a. **The foundational attribute** which compels Warriors to do what they do (including God the Father and Christ Jesus the Son) is _____!

    b. **How _is_ the Warrior-Spirit compatible with a *mature* Christian worldview?**

4. a. **Review the verses on Page 209-210. Why do God the Father, Christ Jesus, and the Epistles (New Testament Letters) zealously *safeguard* the integrity of the Lord's *Warrior Culture*?**

    b. <u>READ:</u> Matthew 8:18-22, Luke 16:13, Matthew 10:21-28, 1 Corinthians 5:9-13, 6:9-11, Ephesians 5:1-11, 1 Thessalonians 4:1-8, Romans 6:17-18, Philippians 1:27-30, Philippians 2:1-11, Hebrews 10:19-25, 2 Timothy 1:6-10, 2:3-7, Colossians 3:15-17

What are some of the "cultural expectations" that are laid out for us at our *"Kingdom Indoc"* (Salvation/Conversion)?

5. In times of difficulty, trials, testing, and suffering, to what does your *"Spiritual Muscle Memory"* resort (p. 211)? [Examples: Resentment, Fear, Victimization, Sadness, Self-loathing, Anger, Anxiety …or…Prayer, Trust, Hope, Fasting, Thanksgiving, God's Promises, Surrenderedness, Quietness, Tenacity, Comfort, etc.]

MOTTO: "SEMPER FIDELIS"

6. a. Read the verses on Pages 216-218: Describe why the Warrior Class of the Lord *has/can have* an *"Invincibility Complex"* as we walk out our Faith.

   b. IT IS NOT ABOUT THE _____ OF YOUR _____,

      IT IS ABOUT THE _____ OF YOUR _____!

   c. WE FIGHT _____

      NOT _____!

IDIOM: "SUCK IT UP!"

7. **Read:** Jeremiah 12:5, Isaiah 7:9b, Proverbs 24:10, Hebrews 10:35-36, James 1:12, 1 Timothy 6:12, Revelation 3:8-13

Where is the Lord of Heaven's Armies *lovingly* calling you to *"suck it up"* this very day?

Why is He calling you to this?

MOTTO: "GET IN THE FIGHT"

8. a. Our Christian calling demands we remain _____ and _____

_____ in the spiritual battle against both _____ and our _____

_____ (p. 223).

b. Is your faith tested more when you are called to step out in "*action*", or when you are restrained by "*inaction*" (waiting on the Lord)? Why?

c. <u>Fill in the blanks (p. 226)</u>: When weariness and faintness of resolve presents its paralyzing head, admonish one another: "_____"! In the face of battle, remind one another:

"_____"! As the Day of the Lord approaches, charge one another: "_____

_____"! Come fully into the Esprit de Corps of the Lord. Gird up your loins, be prepared for action, and every day and in every way, champion the Ethos of the Warrior Class of the Lord and _____!

MOTTO: "COMPLACENCY KILLS"

4. a. Define:

COMPLACENCY: *noun*

b. **Why is the Warrior Class motto of "Complacency Kills"** so crucial for the People of God to understand? How does our Heavenly Commander-in-Chief deal with complacency on His battlefield?

ESPIRT DE CORPS

10. a. Page 231 of Omega Dynamics states, "Esprit de Corps is one of the single most defining characteristics of a rich Warrior Culture. The brotherhood, comradery, fellowship, and bond forged between the ranks of warriors is something most people, regretfully, will never taste. The nexus of fidelity among the Warrior Class is centered on one crucial truism: mutually-assured sacrifice given in brotherly love. Christ Jesus Himself established the magnitude of this Kingdom Reality when He declared, 'Greater love has no one than this, that someone lay down his life for his friends' (John 15:13)."

Read: John 15:13, Ecclesiastes 4:9-12, Colossians 3:12-17, Ephesians 4:1-16, Ephesians 5:15-21, Philippians 2:1-12, Romans 8:16-17, Colossians 1:22-24, 1 Peter 5:8-11, Philippians 1:27-30, John 13:34-35, 2 Corinthians 1:3-11, 1 Peter 4

Examine your immediate Church Body: Does it possess the hallmarks of rich *Esprit de Corps*? Would you personally be "*authenticated*" as a member of Warrior Class of the Lord by your Esprit de Corps for your brothers and sisters?

b. **How do sufferings and hardships for the cause of Christ and for one another work to produce maturity, unity, joy, and *Authentic Love*? In contrast, what *is* the consequence of Christians remaining comfortable, isolated, or self-preserving in the war that is raging all around us?**

c. **Philippians 1:29 states**, "For to you it has been _**granted**_ on behalf of Christ, not only to believe in Him, but also to suffer for His sake…." **Do you believe that it is a privilege to suffer for the sake of the name of Christ Jesus? WHY or WHY NOT? Where, specifically, can you pray and ask the Lord for greater understanding and freedom in grasping this powerful truth?**

WARRIOR CLASS TACTICS AND STRATEGIES

11. List several amazing aspects of the _Good News_ about the Warrior Class of the Most High (p. 237-241)

    1. _____

    2. _____

    3. _____

    4. _____

    5. _____

12. **Describe where you need to Repent and take up the Ethos of the Warrior Culture of the Lord; where you are going to foster/mature a sincere Warrior-Spirit:**

13. **Describe where the True and Better Warrior Culture which you have been invited into causes you to rejoice and worship the King of Glory; where it spurs on refreshment, confidence, and courage in your identity in Christ:**

14. In deliberate quietness and stillness, prayerfully ask the Lord how He sees you (not how you *feel* He may see you); ask the Lord what it is that He wants to speak over you. <u>WRITE IT BELOW:</u>

15. List where you are going to uphold the expectations of the Warrior Class of the Lord as well as where you are going to advance it forward

 # Battle Plan

OMEGA DYNAMICS FOR ADVANCING ON THE BATTLEFIELD	MY WARRIOR IDENTITY IN CHRIST JESUS

MY WEAPONS [VERSES] TO MEMORIZE:

HOW I WILL TAKE THE FIGHT TO THE ENEMY	MY BATTLEFIELD PRAYER

NOTES

_____

_____

_____

_____

_____

_____

_____

_____

_____

_____

_____

_____

SESSION 9

Counter Insurgency and Asymmetric Warfare

For freedom Christ has set us free; stand firm therefore,
and do not submit again to a yoke of slavery. **Galatians. 5:1**

We Warriors of the Lord must understand our identity as Free Men in order to break the despotism of the Rebel Insurgents. And we must understand the despotism in order to fan into flame the embers of revolution! Until we do this, we cannot emancipate those who remain under the PSYOP (Psychological Operation) that "resistance is futile". As children of light and children of liberty, we Freedom Fighters of God are directed to enter the fray and work to expose the Insurgents' cruel, hidden hand and tactics. Never again will the sting of cold fetters clasping against our flesh be tolerated! !

So if the Son sets you free, you will be free indeed. **John 8:36**

This is the clarion call of the Redeemed; the power of the Warrior Class; this is the ideological foundation of our Counter Insurgency: FREEDOM! Freedom from fear, freedom from the obligation to do what your sinful nature urges you to do; freedom in life and freedom in death; freedom from striving and freedom from basing our hope on worldly validations; freedom from negativity and criticism; freedom to unconditionally love regardless of what is reciprocated; freedom to surrender our sense of worth, status and feeble identities; freedom to stand boldly or to sit patiently; freedom to be pressed on every side, knowing that we will never be crushed; freedom to stumble, knowing He will not let us fall; freedom to suffer and freedom to rejoice; freedom to humble ourselves under the mighty hand of God; freedom in obscurity and freedom in exultation; freedom to speak out and freedom to sit silently in meekness under the reproach of mockers, scoffers, and revilers; and, freedom to fight without restraint! (O.D., p. 255-256)

1. **President John F. Kennedy offered the following insight when speaking to a West Point Academy Graduation in 1962:**

   This is another type of war, new in its intensity, ancient in its origin—war by guerrillas, subversives, insurgents, assassins, war by ambush instead of by combat; by infiltration, instead of aggression, seeking victory by eroding and exhausting the enemy instead of engaging him. . . . It preys on economic unrest and ethnic conflicts. It requires in those situations where we must counter it, and these are the kinds of challenges that will be before us in the next decade if freedom is to be saved, a whole new kind of strategy, a wholly different kind of force, and therefore a new and wholly different kind of military training (p. 243).

In what ways has "*another type of war, new in its intensity, ancient in its origin,*" begun to be waged against the culture, the Nation, the Globe, and the Church in this generation? What is the Biblically-Prophetic significance of the Guerilla Tactics that we are seeing emerge?

[**Read:** Daniel 12:1-4, 2 Timothy 3:1-13, 2 Timothy 4:3-4, 2 Thessalonians 2:5-12, 1 Thessalonians 5:1-5, 2 Peter 2:1-3, 2 Peter 3:3-4, 17, Matthew 24:1-9, 21-24, Luke 21:25-32, Luke 12:42-48, Revelation 12:12, Revelation 17, etc.]

2. **Page 244 states that, "CONVENTIONAL TACTICS AGAINST AN UNCONVENTIONAL ENEMY ENSURES DEFEAT!" List several *Conventional Tactics* regularly being employed by the Church that have led us to the edge of the Great Apostasy (2 Thess 2:3)** (i.e. Hyper-Grace, cultural compromise, "It's not for me to judge", "If we just elect the right people to Government", "It won't happen in my lifetime", etc.)

   a. _____

   b. _____

   c. _____

3. **Page 244. The mandate entrusted to the People of God, the very thrust of our Omega Dynamics: to conduct COIN Ops** (*Counter Insurgency Operations*)

_____

_____

_____

_____

_____!

4. **Page 246 states,** "Is not the cosmic story into which we have been written one of rebellion, oppression, captivity, and bondage juxtaposed to freedom, redemption, regeneration, reconciliation, and rescue from the dominion of Rebellious Insurrection (the Insurrectionists in High Places as well as those of our own flesh)? For this reason, the entire concept of freedom and "Freedom Fighters" is infused within the Word of God! It is foundational to our understanding of the "greater narrative," and the fathomless wonders of the Gospel of Jesus Christ!"

Look at the attributes of a Freedom Fighter (p. 246-248): How is the concept of a *Freedom Fighter* at the heart of the Warrior Class of the Lord? How has Christ Jesus demonstrated that Perfect Example of the True and Better *Freedom Fighter*?

5. **Page 247:** "Freedom Fighters possess a _____ _____ to combat every form of _____ irrespective of the magnitude of _____ required. They cannot capitulate to oppression and tyranny for it is an _____ _____ for freedom and subjugation to _____."

6. **What is the "*BURDEN OF THE WARRIOR CLASS*" that is detailed on Pages 247-248?**

7. The appropriate posture of the Redeemed of the Lord: men and women of violence in "holy contention thrusting [ourselves]" toward the Kingdom of God (p. 251)!

VIOLENT: *synonyms*

8. "When a Warrior steps into combat it is an assumed prerequisite that he or she be a *Man of Violence*. To be anything else, even in its slightest variance, is to become a battlefield casualty who can no longer serve effectually in the furtherance of the mission objectives (p. 249)."

a. **What is your reaction to and/or understanding of the Kingdom Reality that** *"Violence of action wins the day"* **(Matt 11:12)?**

b. **Read the Bible Commentary [*Matthew Henry*] on Matthew 11:12 (p.250-251): How is the calling of a mature Christian to be a "Peacemaker" (Matt 5:5,9) as well as *Men and Women of Violence* reconciled in our mission for the Kingdom of God through Christ Jesus? In other words, in the fight against sin (*within* and *without*) and against the Spiritual Wickedness in High Places, how is *Peace* achieved through our *War*?**

9. Page 251: "Christ Jesus is not only the _____ of the axiom that "violence of action wins the day" (Matt. 11:12), but He is also the _____ _____of it!   He knew and understood what it took to not only win _____ _____, but to win _____ _____ _____ from there on through _____ _____.

10. How did Christ Jesus reconcile *Peace* and *War/Violence* in the fulfillment of His Mission (p. 251-253)?

11. **Page 254 states,** "We must understand this [Rom 8:1-25] Kingdom Reality, Beloved, because the Counter Insurgency can *only* be effectively waged from the position of compulsion which bursts forth from an outflow-understanding of your *freedom*; your freedom in Christ Jesus; freedom to stand unashamed at the Judgment Seat of God; freedom in life (come what may) and freedom in death. And that freedom, the very costly, invaluable freedom bestowed upon us by grace, now obligates *much* in return."

Describe the *burden* of *Freedom* that is in the heart of the Warrior Redeemed. How does/should our *Freedom* compel us to conduct *Counter Insurgency Operations* in this generation (p. 254-255)?

12. *FREEDOM* IS OUR IDENTITY IMMOVABLE: Why?

13. **List several answers to the following questions from Page 257-258 both personally and for the Church as a whole:**

"…why then, do we willingly remain in a counterfeited state of subjugation to the Insurgents? Why, with the most perverse display of Stockholm Syndrome under tyranny, oppression, deception, abuse, and defeatism, do we remain under our Enemies' control matrix? Why are we distrustful of unmitigated *freedom* as we cling to our Oppressor?… Why do so many fear joining the ranks of the *Freedom Fighters* and standing up against Luciferian Totalitarianism?… Why do those who sit under oppression often resent those who, having been freed, fight for the things of God?"

1. _____

2. _____

3. _____

4. _____

5. _____

WARRIOR CLASS TACTICS AND STRATEGIES

1. This is how I am going to personally advance the True and Better Counter Insurgency in this generation. This is how I will be an asset to the Counter Insurgency already in action within the ranks of the Warrior Class of the Lord.

2. <u>Write it down!</u> Where you need to *REPENT* of making little of the *"burden of your Freedom"* through Christ; Discern where the *familiar taunt* of the Oppressor is trying to place you in bondage and *RENOUNCE IT*; <u>Write it down</u>! Identify the cold, rusted fetters (*shackles of imprisonment*) you need to *THROW OFF*; <u>Write them down</u>!

3. **I am waging war** against the Rebel Insurgents in my midst this very day by:

      1. _____

      2. _____

      3. _____

4. <u>**Become**</u> men and women of *violence* and *win the day*!

5. <u>**Fight**</u> for those who remain oppressed and in bondage under the cruel hand of our Insurgent Enemies!

6. <u>**Redeem**</u> the time, for the days are evil!

7. <u>**Look**</u> to the Object of our liberty, Jesus Christ, the Freedom Fighter and Head of the Counter-Insurgency!

8. <u>**Seize**</u> the identity that has been established for us in the Holy Blood of the Lamb and live out from it!

9. <u>**Take**</u> hold of that for which Christ has taken hold of us… freedom… and never let it be snatched away!

10. <u>**Fight**</u> **to the death, whatever it might be, because you have been freed from the fear of** *It [Death]* **altogether!**

Battle Plan

OMEGA DYNAMICS FOR ADVANCING ON THE BATTLEFIELD	MY WARRIOR IDENTITY IN CHRIST JESUS

MY WEAPONS [VERSES] TO MEMORIZE:

HOW I WILL TAKE THE FIGHT TO THE ENEMY	MY BATTLEFIELD PRAYER

NOTES

SESSION 10

Force Multipliers: The Jehoshaphat JDAM

Scripture is replete with the strategic advantages of Worshipful Warriors who inquire of the Lord through prayer, fasting, and unconditional trust. Acting as a Supernatural Force Multiplier, the worship-filled, prostrated hearts and mouths of the People of God exact precise and devastating damage on the Enemy. Nothing achieves such insurmountable advantage over the mighty hordes of Darkness as the surrendered, entrusted, rejoicing heart of the Warrior Redeemed.

Like a JDAM Missile, praise to the Lord takes our "unguided", "dumb bomb" efforts, and converts them into "precision-guided munitions". Our efforts become "upgraded" with the "smart technology" of the Heavenly Hosts as we "resolve to inquire of the Lord". In "resoluteness", we Warring Saints of the Lord take our fighting positions fully outfitted in our battle array and make way for demonstration of Deliverance from the strong right hand of God Almighty. This is how the People of God are to conduct unequalled Asymmetrical Warfare. This is the Weapon and Power by which we come against the throngs of the Insurgent Enemy (O.D., p. 262-263).

Beloved, the Body of Christ must lay hold of the wondrous *Force Multipliers* lavished upon us from our Heavenly Commander-in-Chief! More importantly, we must fix our eyes upon *The Force Multiplier*, Christ Jesus! As we do so in increasing measure, our boldness, steadfast resolve, joy, and overwhelming victory will drive the Enemy from our midst; wherever they may be! It is time to *truly* take hold of that for which Christ Jesus has taken hold of us and stand anew among the Warrior Class of the Most High!

1. a. Look at the definition of a *Force Multiplier* on Page 263. Without reading ahead, list several *Force Multipliers* that the Lord has bestowed upon His redeemed sons and daughters:

    b. As you look at your list above, answer the following questions thoughtfully: Do you regularly *deploy* (make effective use of) these *Force Multipliers* in the fight against wickedness, sin, the flesh, and the Enemies of God? Are you trained/skilled in their deployment? If so, *how* do you; if not, *why* don't you?

2. **Read:** Ephesians 1:3-23, 1 Corinthians 12:4-11, Romans 1:11-12, 2 Peter 1:3-4. 2 Corinthians 6:3-10, 2 Corinthians 10:3-6, 2 Timothy 1:6-8, Colossians 1:13-14, James 5:13-16, Ephesians 6:10-18, John 11:25-26, Hebrews 2:14-15, Matthew 28:18-20, John 15:5-16

    Now describe the *Force Multipliers* that <u>ARE</u> ours through Christ Jesus:

3. Read 2 Chronicles 20: List several Combat Strategies that were used by King Jehoshaphat and the people to ensure battlefield victory against overwhelming odds (what were their *Force Multipliers*)?

    1. _____

    2. _____

    3. _____

    4. _____

    5. _____

4. **Picture your personal *Worst-Case Scenario* <u>physically</u>** (societal collapse, war, famine, persecution, imprisonment, major illness, loss of family, refugee status, etc.) **and <u>spiritually</u>** (despair, longing, grief, shame, back-sliding, demonic oppression and attack, supernatural occurrences, etc.). **Now picture your *every-day* struggles and trials** (physical, relational, marital, work, church conduct, etc.).

Answer the following with thoughtfulness: What do you *"resolve"* to do when a vast *"army"* more powerful than yourself is attacking (2 Chron 20:3); what has your spiritual *"muscle memory"* been trained to do?

[**<u>Examples</u>**: cut and run, fear, anxiousness, racing thoughts, anger, resentment, victim mentality, despair, self-reliance, grit teeth and fight, **<u>or</u>** trust, pray, fast, become quieted, worship, surrender, be bold, courageous, steadfast, immovable, hopeful, etc.]

5. **<u>Read</u>:** 1 Samuel 23:1-5, 10-14, 1 Samuel 30:7-8, 2 Samuel 2:1-2, 2 Kings 22:11-13, 18-20, Isaiah 30:15, Exodus 14:13-14, Joshua 6:1-5, Psalm 27:14, Psalm 37:1-9, Philippians 3:1, Philippians 4:4-6, 1 Corinthians 15:58, Philippians 1:27-28, Ephesians 6:10-13, 1 Corinthians 16:13, Psalm 91:14-16, Malachi 4:2-3, Psalm 112:1-8

What attributes comprise the *muscle memory* of the Warrior Class of the Lord?

6. **<u>Force Multiplier: Battlefield Comms</u>**

Page 270 states: "We are commanded to commune with the Lord; to Tabernacle with Him, and to be found dwelling, abiding, and hiding in Him for this very reason: to live, move, and act *out from* His wisdom, power, and purposes. 'Pray without ceasing' has been issued as our charge (1 Thes 5:16-18). Put on the Armor of God, 'And pray in the Spirit on all occasions with all kinds of prayers and requests...[and] be alert and always keep on praying for all the Lord's people' is our command (Eph 6:18). We are exhorted and encouraged that the Lord is near to those who call on Him and He acts on their behalf (Ps 145:18, James 4:8). When we pray (out of a surrendered, increasingly-sanctified life) things happen! They happen on a multi-dimensional level as assets are shifted, troop movements are coordinated, resupply is set in motion, and Close-Air-Support is directed to our positions!

Like Elisha peering into the unseen realm and seeing the Armies of Heaven in battle formation, our communion with the Lord instills an incomparable bravery in us; He gives His servants real-time intelligence, discernment, and reinforcement-of-courage in the face of our Enemies. The Weary-Warriors of God often need reminding of the vast Heavenly Force Multipliers always on 'stand by.'"

a. **Describe the True and Better Comms of the Warrior Class (p. 268): Where is it found? How is it maintained? What is the *strategic* value of "good-to-go" Comms for the Redeemed of the Lord?**

b. **Page 272-273 states,** "The Enemy is waging Cyberwarfare against the People of God with zealous determination. Everything in *their* arsenal is designed to disrupt and corrupt our Communion, our Comms. We had better harden our 'information technology' networks ASAP! Purge the sin, distractions, anemic excuses, worldly thinking, and the doublemindedness that leaves us exposed and confused in the fog of war. As the Warrior Class of the Most High, we must hunger and thirst for righteousness so that our prayers *will be* powerful, effectual, and availing much; so that *we are* Force Multipliers for one another in the days ahead! All of us Saints, to the individual, better be on our spiritual 'A-Game'. We should have the expectancy that when we intercede for one another, when we coordinate our prayers from the trenches of this war, the spectacular precision of *Heavenly Air Assets* will be inbound! The Mission of the Kingdom of God and the yet unredeemed people of the world demand it!"

Give an evaluation:

How is your personal, intimate Communion with the Lord? What is disrupting/corrupting your Comms? Do you have a reputation of having *"powerful and effectual"* prayers? Can your Brothers and Sisters have an expectancy that you are on your *spiritual "A-Game"*? Are you *Resolute* in seeking the Lord's face? Do you study Jesus to grow in *knowing* of the True and Better Warrior Class?

7. <u>Force Multiplier: Worshipping Warriors</u>

a. **Page 274-275 exhorts:** "Like a rallying cry on the field of battle, worshipful hearts of men and women champion the fame of the Lord Most High. The song of the Redeemed diminishes all confidence in the *flesh* and our own strength (self) and, instead, exalts the might of our Warring King….

The reason it is such a dynamic Force Multiplier is because it champions God's glory instead of our own. It reveals trust, hope, humility, and our dependency on Him. A Warrior's worship arrests a tumultuous, fearful, or anxious heart and returns it to a submissive 'surrenderedness' to the Lord. This is why we often see in Scripture the *imperative* to "praise the Lord". As if to regain dominion over our timorous, prideful, or wayward hearts, the Psalmists teach us to command our faculties to reverently worship: "Bless the Lord, O my soul" (Ps 103:1-2). Rejoicing opens the door to the blessings bestowed on the humble and contrite in heart (Ps.138:6; Prov. 3:34, 29:23; Matt 23:12; Luke 1:52; James 4:6) and cultivates that "quietness and trust" wherein we find our strength (Isa. 30:15)."

Do you view worship/praise/thanksgiving as a *Supernatural Weapon of Warfare*? Why is it of such powerful, strategic importance to "rejoice always"? What does a worshipful heart communicate to the Enemy as well as to the Lord Whom you proclaim?

b. **Read:** Job 1:13-22, Habakkuk 3:17-19, Psalm 138:7-8, Lamentation 3:1-33, 2 Chronicles 20:15-18, Luke 10:17-20, 1 Peter 1:3-9, Acts 5:40-42, Hebrews 10:32-39, 2 Corinthians 12:9-10, James 1:2-4, Psalm 121, Numbers 23:19, Hebrews 13:8, John 4:23-24

Why can you (why *must* you) be a Worshipping Warrior?

8. <u>Force Multiplier: Coalition Forces</u>

a. **Read:** 2 Kings 6:15-17, Isaiah 35:3-4, and Romans 15:1-2

As a member of the True and Better *Multidimensional Coalition* how do you "spur on" the weak and wayward in heart? Do you call them <u>OUT</u>, or do you call them <u>UP</u>? What are the Eternal Truths (our identity and hope in Christ Jesus) that you preach to yourself and to others while in this theater of war (p. 278-280)?

b. **Page 280 states,** "We are each other's Force Multiplier" and "War necessitates a *strong, unified* Coalition."

Would you stand confidently and boldly in the face of physical [real], emotional, or supernatural warfare with the Body (Sold-out Believers in Christ Jesus) with whom you <u>*regularly*</u> fellowship and who currently surrounds you? Where do you need to spur one another on? In what ways can you increasingly be an asset to your *Spiritual Platoon* and *Fire Team* in this generation?

c. **Page 279 states,** "The Lord always, always, *always* has a 'ram in the bush' (Gen 22). The Lord *always* has a remnant. And the strength of the Remnant of the Lord cannot be minimized, vilified, denigrated, or diminished. Because it is *His* remnant! Regardless of our perception, 'those who are with us are more than those who are with them'...always and without fail. As with the nation of Israel, Gideon's 300, and 12 'unlearned' young men, you and I bear witness to what God Almighty can do with a surrendered, obedient few in this day and time!"

What is the result of "A Few Good Men" who are radically surrendered to the Lord? Are you willing to be counted among the Warrior Class of the Lord? Where does your identity in Christ Jesus need *shoring-up* **for you to** *step up* **and** *step out* **in this war of the Ages?**

9. <u>Force Multiplier: The Warrior Worm</u>

a. **Describe how having an accurate self-perception of our true state [*lowly* and *weak*] before a Holy and Awesome God makes room for the greatest Force Multiplier of all: the strong right arm of the Lord.**

[**Read:** 1 Corinthians 10:12, 2 Corinthians 12:7-10, Isaiah 66:1-2, Isaiah 64:4-6, Isaiah 42:8, Ephesians 2:4-10, 1 Corinthians 1:26-31, 1 Peter 2:9, John 15:16, 2 Thessalonians 2:13-17]

b. **Reread 1 Corinthians 1:26-31: Take an account of your own life as well as the Church Body to which you belong. Are you operating out from the Lord's Upside-Down Kingdom, or are you walking in agreement with the Kingdom-Builders of the World?** [Note: This is often best discerned by examining your internal *posture*: Is it self-reliant, calculated, protective, security/financial-driven, success/accomplishment/influence-oriented **or** is it quieted, open-handed, humble, trusting, faith-based?]

c. **Page 284 states,** "By affirming that he is 'little' and a 'worm', the Lord is effectually speaking peace, security, and a spirit of fearlessness over him [Jacob]. It is the amazing assurance that Jacob brings absolutely nothing to the table and nothing to the fight. Therefore, all efforts, all battles, and all outcomes are solely dependent on the Lord. It serves to disarm Israel (Jacob) of his pride, anxious wonderings, and self-exaltation (even if only for a moment) as it reminds him of his standing before his Holy Father. It is only once we accept our 'knighting' into 'Wormhood' that we become an open conduit for the demonstration of God's power before both a formidable Foe and a dying world."

Read: Galatians 6:9, 1 Peter 5:6, Lamentations 3:24-33, Psalm 33:18-22, Psalm 44:6-8, Isaiah 31:1-3, Jeremiah 17:5-8, Isaiah 30:15-17, Isaiah 40:27-31, Jeremiah 2:5-6, 13, Psalm 40:1-5, Revelation 3:17-18, Hebrews 10:38

What is your response to being an "*appendage-less, little worm*"? Do you *willingly* come under the mighty hand of the Lord or do you resent/resist your estate? Do you seek carnal-Force Multipliers to "make things happen" or do you wait on and hope in the Lord? Would you be considered *accursed* or *blessed* (Jere 17:5-8)?

d. "*BECOMING AN APPENDAGE-LESS WORM BEFORE THE LORD IS A STRATEGIC ACT OF WAR!... To be a worm is to be endeared to the Lord. To be a worm is to become fearless and peace-filled. To be a worm is to become a Warrior who lives, moves, and has our being in the powerful Force Multiplication of the Most High (p. 289)!*"

List Courses of Action you are going to take in order to make way for the *Force Multiplier* of the strong right arm of the Lord.

1. _____

2. _____

3. _____

10. The end of Chapter 10 puts forth this challenge:

I pray that the Warrior Remnant of the Lord would "paint" the Insurgent targets in our lives with the laser of a Jehoshaphat JDAM. Do this and see what happens! Show up to the fight and see what happens! Let us *resolve* to inquire of the Lord, prostrate ourselves to Him, fill our hearts and homes with praise as Worshipping Warriors, commune with the Lord constantly, *and see what happens*! Let us deploy the gracious Force Multipliers of the Kingdom of God, fix our eyes on *The Force Multiplier, Christ Jesus Himself*, and proclaim, "*Take up your positions; stand firm and see the deliverance the Lord will give you!*"

Where are you going to take the fight right to the Enemy and let loose the precision-guided munitions of our *Heavenly Air Assets* (in your heart and against abounding lawlessness)?

WARRIOR CLASS TACTICS AND STRATEGIES

1. **Stop** *Carpet Bombing* the Insurgents that are assaulting you, your Church Body, this Nation, and the Globe and begin loosing *Precision-Guided Munitions* from on High!

2. **Take the fight** to the Enemy (Eph. 6:12) by deploying Imprecatory Prayers: Psalms 5, 7, 17, 35, 37, 55, 58, 59, 69, 70, 83, 107:39-43, 109, 139, and others.

3. ***Resolve*** to inquire of the Lord always, and diligently work to guard your Comms (Communion) with the Lord Most High.

4. "**Pray without ceasing**" (1 Thess 5:16-18) and access the Force Multipliers of the Lord of the Heaven's Armies.

5. ***Dwell, Seek, Hide In, Abide By, Commune and Tabernacle*** with the Lord Jesus Christ so that you can stand/withstand in the days ahead.

6. ***Command*** your soul to "Praise the Lord" and "rejoice always". Champion the glory of God the Father and our Warrior King, Jesus Christ, by the worship of your heart in all things. This is a precision *kill-shot* to any Enemy and an affirmation of the supremacy of Christ over all!

7. ***Be the Body*****!** Get on your "Spiritual A-Game", put on your Armor (the Gospel of Jesus Christ), stand shoulder-to-shoulder with those of a Warrior-Spirit, and advance the Kingdom of God!

8. **Receive** your estate as a "worm" with gladness and move out from God's *might, power, provision, abilities, resources, promises, hope, love,* and *Eternal Victory*!

9. ***REPENT*** **and** ***SURRENDER*** where you have sought to make alliances with Men (your own self-reliance included), where you have cast off the easy yoke of the Lord, or become resentful, impatient, embittered, joyless, etc. Commit anew to your Good, Worthy, All-Powerful Commander-in-Chief.

10. **Inquire** of the Lord, sing to Him from your heart, put on your Kit (Armor), advance with a confident-fierceness on the battlefield, and watch what ***the Lord*** will do!

11. **USE** the dynamically-superior *Force Multipliers* you have been "*issued*" through Christ Jesus in this War of the Ages.

Battle Plan

OMEGA DYNAMICS FOR ADVANCING ON THE BATTLEFIELD	MY WARRIOR IDENTITY IN CHRIST JESUS

MY WEAPONS [VERSES] TO MEMORIZE:

HOW I WILL TAKE THE FIGHT TO THE ENEMY	MY BATTLEFIELD PRAYER

NOTES

_____

_____

_____

_____

_____

_____

_____

_____

_____

_____

_____

_____

SESSION 11

Weapons of Warfare:
The Armor (Kit) of God

The weapons of the Warrior Saints of the Most High are not weak because they are not made by Man; instead, they are mighty, through God, to the destroying of every stronghold and every false pretense that sets itself up against the knowledge of God. We are to employ them in the advancement of the Kingdom in demonstration of that might! Never are our swords to be sheathed or our rifles slung upon our shoulders but with both hands we cleave to our weapons. And by their constant use we appropriate our directive as those who are more than conquerors. This only bursts forth from a profound knowing of Who has issued these Weapons and Who has conferred upon us overwhelming Victory...

This is why the Weapons of our Warfare are superior in every way: it is literally Christ in us! Christ, the Word made flesh; the Word, the Sword of the Spirit; the Sword we are to take hold of and wield as the eternal, all powerful Weapon of Mass Destruction against the Lawless Rebels within our flesh and the Lawless Rebels in high places! By prayer, confession, repentance, worship, fellowship, sanctification, the wielding of the Sword of the Word, and humble obedience to the Captain of our Salvation, the Warring Saints of the Lord advance the Kingdom of God in overwhelming victory! (O.D., p. 313-317)

1. **Page 293 states,** "Our Mission is to war alongside Christ Jesus to save souls, redeeming what has been corrupted, and in order to do so successfully, we absolutely must know the weight of the Whole Armor of God upon our shoulders and in our hands."

a. What have you been taught regarding the *Armor of God*; how has its "weight" and "merit" been presented to you? Explain your understanding of why it is needed and against whom it is to be used (Ephesians 6:10-20)?

b. What does the issuance of this *Armor* tell us about the nature of the Christian calling and life?

2. **Page 293:** "With _____ sight, our appearance needs to be that of '_____ - _____' for the Kingdom of God, equipped to _____ house-to-house, inflicting _____ _____on the Enemy Insurgents."

3. Give several reasons why understanding the power and purpose of the *Whole Kit of God* is crucial for the Warrior Class of the Lord (p. 294-297):

4. a. What is the reciprocal role of the Kit of God (p. 296-297)?

    b. What happens in the heart and spirit of Warriors when their *Kit* is donned (put on)? Is this your posture as you walk in faith and advance the Kingdom of God; the posture of your Church Body? WHY or WHY NOT?

5. List 3 truths that impacted you from C.H. Spurgeon's 1891 Sermon on Pages 297-298:

   1. _____

   2. _____

   3. _____

6. Page 300-302

THE POWER AND PURPOSE OF MY KIT

7. <u>Read:</u> Colossians 1:13-14, 2:15, Hebrews 12:18-29, John 14:12-21, Luke 10:19, Romans 8:28-38

a. What is being declared to us about the eternal power of our Kit, literally Christ in us?

b. "Christ is in the Father, we are in Christ, and Christ is in us! _____, these Weapons

   of Warfare and Armor of God _____ to us are _____

   to do something!"

c. What are you doing with your *Weapons* and *Armor* (Eph 5:8-17)? How is it being worn? In what ways is it being deployed?

8. **Page 304 states:** "…the Word of Christ Jesus and the eternal words of the Epistles exhort and admonish us that the nature of the Christian Life is one of hostility. It is waged by the Blood-Bought Saints through tenacious truth, love, hope, and action coming from their eternally secure identity in Christ! It is waged in preaching the totality of the Kingdom of God (not just comfort in Salvation). From sun up to sun down, and every second in between, every action or lack thereof is viewed in the Heavenlies as an act of war. It matters little if you perceive it or agree with it, it just *is*."

Detail the <u>*Acts of War*</u> by a mature Christian, and their respective <u>*Combat Effects*</u> from Page 304:

ACT OF WAR	COMBAT EFFECT

9. a. **Page 306:** "…our ultimate WMD (Weapon of Mass Destruction) in the War of the Ages is the Word of the Lord.

It is the Weapon of Mass _____ ,

Weapon of Mass _____ ,

Weapon of Mass _____ ,

Weapon of Mass _____ ,

Weapon of Mass _____ ,

and Weapon of Mass _____ **over all the powers of the Enemy!**

b. Why?

10. **Page 306 states,** "To take hold of this Sword, to clutch it in both hands with great vigor, and to wield it with tremendous skill is a *breathtaking* and fearful thing. However, to wield this Sword in error, without thorough training, or to leave it all-together sheathed as an ornament around your waist is an equally *awful* and dreadful thing."

After having read the details of our WMD, the Sword [Word] of the Lord, how intimately have you known Its *weight* in your hand? How have you wielded the Sword of the Lord? How would both Friend and Foe describe you on the field of battle?

11. **Review Pages 307-308. List 10 Attributes/Effects of the Sword [Word] of the Spirit:**

1.	6.
2.	7.
3.	8.
4.	9.
5.	10.

12. "There is nothing more terrifying or devastating to the Enemy than a man or woman of the Lord who knows and obeys the Word of God (p. 309)."

Read: 1 Samuel 13:13-14, 19-22, Psalm 78:8-10, Haggai 1:3-11, 2 Timothy 4:1-4, 2 Peter 3:1-3, 2 Corinthians 2:17, Isaiah 30:9-13, Jeremiah 6:10, Jeremiah 8:4-9, Jeremiah 25:4-7, Deuteronomy 6:1-9, John 6:56-67

Describe the consequences of *NOT knowing/taking* the Sword [the Word]. How is it to the Enemy's *tactical advantage* to reduce your value, hunger, dependency, equipping, training, and delight in the Word of the Lord?

13. **Page 312 states,** "Weapon of Mass Destruction; this is the power of the Word in us! Take It from Its sheath and never put It back! Stop dragging It on the rocks behind you like resentful, reluctant conscripts who are weak and weary from Its weight. Stop adorning your fireplace with It, where It remains ornamentally gleaming, free of the wear-marks of war! If this is what you have done, repent; turn back to the refreshing, life-giving, empowering, refining Word and train anew with It! 'Today, if you hear His voice, do not harden your hearts' (Heb 4:7)! Your future, the future of your children, and the future of the Church depend upon it!"

Where repentance is needed (with regard to how you have handled your *Sword*), write it in a prayer to the Lord below. Additionally, offer thanksgiving for the grace lavished on you by the Captain of our Salvation:

14. "How we view, understand, and employ what Christ's death and resurrection has afforded us affects every detail of our lives. It affects how we love, fight, endure, persevere, perceive, pray, serve, worship, suffer, hope, and overcome. To know and understand our Weapons of Warfare, and why we can wield them so confidently is to make much of Christ Jesus and seize God's Peace that truly does surpass all understanding (p. 313)."

<u>Read the verses listed on Pages 313-316</u>; these are the Eternal Truths of the Warrior Class. This *Heavenly Armory* from which we draw our weapons: the completed work of Christ over us, in us, and through us!

With _____ we proclaim, "We do not fight _____ a position of victory, but we fight _____ a position of victory!

15. **Ask the Lord to wash over you anew with a** *rightly* **placed** *Warrior-Spirit.* **Below, write a prayer of thanksgiving and worship to our Good King out from that renewed spirit and understanding. Where you desire more of Him,** *tell Him.* **Where you long to make much of the Warrior Class to which you have been called,** *tell Him.* **And where you want to strike a blow against the Enemy in the name of Jesus,** *DO IT!*

WARRIOR CLASS TACTICS AND STRATEGIES

The Omega Dynamics for Chapter 7 are simple yet powerful: *GET LOCKED ON AND GET IN THE FIGHT!* It is your calling, election, and enlistment as a Redeemed Warrior of the Most High. Solidify the identity that is yours through Christ Jesus and His completed work, exemplified by both the *Empty Cross* and the *Empty Tomb*.

1. <u>Renew</u> your *perspective* and *posture* as a mighty warrior, adorned in your *Kit*, advancing across the field of battle in which Victory has been assured *regardless* of your current status (young/old, strong/infirm, influential/obscure, rich/poor, bold/timid, educated/simple, zealous/weary).

2. <u>Know</u> that your *Kit* is the power of Christ *over* you and *in* you and live out from it every day of your life!

3. <u>Employ</u> your *Kit* for what it is designed (**Defends so that you can Offend**) and start *Kicking-Doors* in your flesh, home, church Bodies, and against wickedness in this Evil Age (Gal 1:3-4).

4. <u>Know</u> that to be a Christian is to be a *Warrior* and act like it…. PERIOD!

5. <u>Reject</u> the spirit of passivity, indifference, and apathy coming from many Church leaders and teachers. Fellowship with those of a Warrior-Spirit and call others up into their True and Better Identity in Christ.

6. <u>Renounce</u> any form of a "*victim-mentality*", come out from behind your shield, *fix* your eyes on your Warrior-King, and *get in the fight*!

7. <u>Know</u> the weight of your Kit, the weapons of warfare that are attached to it, and by the power of the Gospel announced to you through the Word and Spirit of Christ Jesus, go to war!

8. <u>Take</u> the Sword of the Spirit, the Word of God, from Its sheath and train vigorously with It! Never put It back, never allow Its edges to become dull, never allow Its glint in the sun to cease!

9. <u>Study and know</u> the WMDs of our *Heavenly Armory* that **ARE** bestowed upon the Warrior Redeemed by the promises of God Almighty. Commit them to memory, store them in your heart, and wield them expertly daily!

10. <u>Fix</u> your identity on Christ Jesus, your victorious, Conquering King alone and stand firm until the end, whatever it may be!

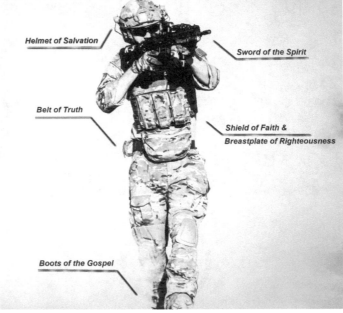

 # Battle Plan

OMEGA DYNAMICS FOR ADVANCING ON THE BATTLEFIELD	MY WARRIOR IDENTITY IN CHRIST JESUS

MY WEAPONS [VERSES] TO MEMORIZE:

HOW I WILL TAKE THE FIGHT TO THE ENEMY	MY BATTLEFIELD PRAYER

NOTES

_____

_____

_____

_____

_____

_____

_____

_____

_____

_____

_____

_____

_____

SESSION 12

Raise The Standard:
To Those Who Overcome

Make no doubt about it, we are at war! By the very cosmic, comprehensive, and absolute nature of this war, we have been conscripted, consigned, and mandated to fight. The only choice left to enlistees is on which side they will fight; whether they are honored unto commendation or defeated unto condemnation. The Glory and Holiness of His Namesake ensures with certainty that He will accept nothing apart from "Unconditional Defeat" of the Rebel Insurgents through the "Unconditionally Surrendered" hearts of the Warriors within His Ranks (O.D., p. 333)…

*Live and conduct yourself in a way that honors the legacy of the Warrior Culture into which you have been adopted by Grace. Do so with such boldness that those around you will be astonished and take note that you have been with Jesus (Acts 4:1-31). Live in hope, love, peace, quietness of spirit, unity, and humility as well as strength, power, boldness, confidence, and fearlessness as you move in faith unto action (Phil 2:1-13), never forgetting that "this is eternal life, that they **know** You, the only true God, and Jesus Christ Whom You have sent" (John 17:3). These are the hallmarks of the Warrior Class! These are the hallmarks of the Redeemed! (O.D., p. 336)*

1. **Page 321** speaks of the significant and intrinsic power of a Battle Standard in that:

This regalia is to be guarded at all cost. It is to be upheld and standing tall at all cost. Its colorful display is to be advancing forward at all cost; never to be lowered or surrendered, even unto death. This demonstrates the powerful, effectual nature of a Standard being raised in battle.

Many, many men have lost their lives to ensure their Colors remained intact and unfurled. Many, many other men willingly threw down their weapons to take charge of their Banner, advancing it with great selfless sacrifice unto their assured peril. This was done time after time, battle after battle, one fallen Color-Bearer after another…because those who understand the nature of the conflict in which they are engaged also understand the gravity of their Banner's *far greater* significance.

After reviewing Pages 320-323 list 8 EFFECTS or ATTRIBUTES of a Battle Standard being unfurled in combat:

THE BATTLE STANDARD

1.	5.
2.	6.
3.	7.
4.	8.

2. **Describe how the Lord Almighty, Jehovah-Nissi, is the True and Better Battle Flag under which the Redeemed of the Lord fight:**

3. **Page 324 states,** "All throughout the earth, the trumpet's blast and the bugler's call have broken the silence of the tense air. The Honor Guard of the Most High has stepped-off, steadfastly advancing the Colors forward in fervent proclamation that the Battle (the climatic, convergent Battle) is now absolute. Therefore, as 'Good Soldiers of Christ', we must close ranks, steady our hearts, and engage the Enemy fearlessly in the unshakable knowing that the Banner of the Lord over us is love (Song 2:4)!"

Read: Isaiah 59:19, Isaiah 31:9, Psalm 20:5-8, Psalm 60:4, Psalm 94:16, Ephesians 5:8-16, 2 Peter 3:8-13, 1 Timothy 6:11-16, Revelation 12:11, Hebrews 10:36-39, Amos 3:8, Proverbs 28:1, 2 Timothy 1:7, Daniel 11:32b

What is the response of the Warrior Class to this good news of our Banner being unfurled from on High? What should our efforts, actions, focus, and posture be as the days advance?

4. **Omega Dynamics exhorts:**

Fight for each other's hearts and minds, our homes and our loved ones; fight against those things seen and unseen, natural and supernatural. Fight the sin that so easily hinders us and fight the fear that beckons us again under its tormenting hand and oppressive bondage. Fight diligently to keep our eyes fixed on Christ Jesus and, in equal fervency, to put to death the temporal pursuits of this world. Fight for the weak and oppressed in spirit; fight for Truth and Justice to ring loudly. In prayer, fight. Through communion and fellowship, fight for one another's freedom. Fight with a worshipful, rejoicing, thankful heart. Make war in the public forums, armed with the Sword of the Spirit and the Spirit of Truth; make way for the demonstration of the power and Spirit of the Lord (1 Cor 2:4, 4:20)! Fight with tenacity until the end, knowing that those who endure **_will_** receive the Crown of Life.

Do this because Christ Jesus already demonstrated the power and endurance with which He was (and is) willing to fight for us… because He endured to the end and is the One Who now _bestows_ the Crown of Life! (p. 325-326)

Have you come to _know_ your Lord and Savior, Jesus Christ, to the degree that you are willing to pay the ultimate sacrifice [bodily death] for both Truth and Authentic Love? Would you today, be unashamed of the Gospel of Jesus unto the death? Are you willing to fight for your children and grandchildren? Would you today, stand up in the assembly of the people and proclaim the righteousness of God?

If not, write your prayer and petition to our loving, tender, patient, and gracious Father where your heart needs encouragement:

5. **I rejoice that I have been foreknown "for such a time as this". I will increasingly make myself ready for the Lord's soon Return and for that _Great Harvest_ that is before me by:**

    1. _____
    2. _____
    3. _____
    4. _____
    5. _____

6. These are the things I call to mind about my Good, Conquering King, the *Object* of my faith on which I will fix my eyes, and therefore I will not lose heart:

THEREFORE I DO NOT LOSE HEART...

7. Here is what You have promised to those "who overcome", Lord (p.330-332):

...TO THOSE WHO OVERCOME

1.	5.
2.	6.
3.	7.
4.	8.

8. This is the *Living Hope*, Christ <u>in</u> me, from which I *boldly* march forward into combat:

1 PETER 1:3-9

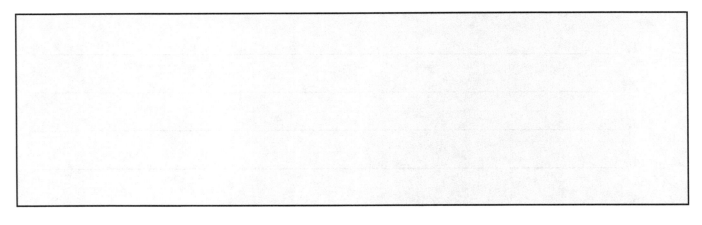

9. These are the Ethos of my identity in Christ Jesus as a Redeemed Warrior of the Most High that I will live by:

THE ETHOS OF MY WARRIOR SPIRIT

1.
2.
3.
4.
5.

10. As I have increased in a *knowing* of the Lord and standing as a Warrior within His ranks, this is the song of praise in my heart:

OH LORD...

11. These are the verses that have helped the most to solidify my Warrior-Spirit: (Choose Several)

12. I will train and be a *Force Multiplier* to the *True and Better Counter Insurgency* by:

13. As a Warrior in a Kingdom that cannot be shaken, these are *my OMEGA DYNAMICS* for the days ahead:

MY OMEGA DYNAMICS

14. Answer the following:

CHRIST JESUS IS THE TRUE AND BETTER WARRIOR BECAUSE HE...

...THEREFORE I AM A WARRIOR!

15. THESE ARE THE WAYS I HAVE BEEN STRENGTHENED AND EQUIPPED FOR THE DAYS AHEAD:

16. Because of my overwhelming victory in Christ, my secure identity in Christ, and the compulsion of Authentic Love that I have been shown through Christ, *I WILL NOW* wake war against the Rebel Insurgency by…

Final Blessings And Prayers

Of this Gospel I was made a minister according to the gift of God's grace, which was given me by the working of His power. To me, though I am the very least of all the saints, this grace was given, to preach to the Gentiles the unsearchable riches of Christ, and to bring to light for everyone what is the plan of the mystery hidden for ages in God, Who created all things, so that through the church the manifold wisdom of God might now be made known to the rulers and authorities in the heavenly places. This was according to the eternal purpose that He has realized in Christ Jesus our Lord, in whom we have boldness and access with confidence through our faith in Him.

…For this reason I bow my knees before the Father, from Whom every family in heaven and on earth is named, that according to the riches of His glory He may grant you to be strengthened with power through His Spirit in your inner being, so that Christ may dwell in your hearts through faith—that you, being rooted and grounded in love, may have strength to comprehend with all the saints what is the breadth and length and height and depth, and to know the love of Christ that surpasses knowledge, that you may be filled with all the fullness of God.

Now to Him Who is able to do far more abundantly than all that we ask or think, according to the power at work within us, to Him be glory in the church and in Christ Jesus throughout all generations, forever and ever. Amen. **Ephesians 3:7-21**

For this reason, ever since I heard about your faith in the Lord Jesus and your love for all the saints, I have not stopped giving thanks for you, remembering you in my prayers. I keep asking that the God of our Lord Jesus Christ, the glorious Father, **may give you the Spirit of wisdom and revelation,** <u>**so that**</u> **you may know him better. I pray also that the eyes of your heart may be enlightened in order that you may know the hope to which He has called you, the riches of His glorious inheritance in the saints, and His incomparably great power for us who believe.** *That power is like the working of His mighty strength, which He exerted in Christ when He raised Him from the dead and seated Him at His right hand in the heavenly realms, far above all rule and authority, power and dominion, and every title that can be given, not only in the present age but also in the one to come. And God placed all things under His feet and appointed Him to be head over everything for the church, which is His body, the fullness of Him Who fills everything in every way.* **Ephesians 1:15-23**

*...since the day we heard about you, **we have not stopped praying for you and asking God to fill you with the knowledge of His will through all spiritual wisdom and understanding. And we pray this in order that you may live a life worthy of the Lord and may please Him in every way:** bearing fruit in every good work, growing in the knowledge of God, being strengthened with all power according to His glorious might so that you may have great endurance and patience, and joyfully giving thanks to the Father, Who has qualified you to share in the inheritance of the saints in the kingdom of light. For He has rescued us from the dominion of darkness and brought us into the kingdom of the Son He loves, in Whom we have redemption, the forgiveness of sins.* **Colossians 1:3-14**

May the God of endurance and encouragement grant you to live in such harmony with one another, in accord with Christ Jesus, that together you may with one voice glorify the God and Father of our Lord Jesus Christ.... May the God of hope fill you with all joy and peace in believing, so that by the power of the Holy Spirit you may abound in hope. **Romans 15:5-6, 13**

*I always thank God for you because of His grace given you in Christ Jesus. For in Him you have been enriched in every way— in all your speaking and in all your knowledge— because our testimony about Christ was confirmed in you. **Therefore you do not lack any spiritual gift as you eagerly wait for our Lord Jesus Christ to be revealed. He will keep you strong to the end, so that you will be blameless on the day of our Lord Jesus Christ. God, Who has called you into fellowship with his Son Jesus Christ our Lord, is faithful.*** **1 Corinthians 1:4-9**

I thank my God every time I remember you. In all my prayers for all of you, I always pray with joy because of your partnership in the gospel from the first day until now, being confident of this, that He Who began a good work in you will carry it on to completion until the day of Christ Jesus.... And this is my prayer: that your love may abound more and more in knowledge and depth of insight, so that you may be able to discern what is best and may be pure and blameless until the day of Christ, filled with the fruit of righteousness that comes through Jesus Christ—to the glory and praise of God. **Philippians 1:3-6, 9-11**

May God Himself, the God of peace, sanctify you through and through. May your whole spirit, soul and body be kept blameless at the coming of our Lord Jesus Christ. The One Who calls you is faithful and He will do it. **1 Thessalonians 5:23-24**

And pray that we may be delivered from wicked and evil men, for not everyone has faith. But the Lord is faithful, and He will strengthen and protect you from the evil one. We have confidence in the Lord that you are doing and will continue to do the things we command. May the Lord direct your hearts into God's love and Christ's perseverance. **2 Thessalonians 3:2-5**

Devote yourselves to prayer, being watchful and thankful. And pray for us, too, that God may open a door for our message, so that we may proclaim the mystery of Christ, for which I am in chains. Pray that I may proclaim it clearly, as I should. **Colossians 4:2-4**

Pray also for me, that whenever I open my mouth, words may be given me so that I will fearlessly make known the mystery of the gospel, for which I am an ambassador in chains. Pray that I may declare it fearlessly, as I should. **Ephesians 6:19-20**

*Lastly, …"Whatever happens, conduct yourselves in a manner worthy of the gospel of Christ. Then, whether I come and see you or only hear about you in my absence, I will know that you stand firm in the one Spirit, striving together as one for the faith of the gospel **without** being frightened in any way by those who oppose you. This is a sign to them that they will be destroyed, but that you will be saved—and that by God. For it has been granted to you on behalf of Christ not only to believe in Him, but also to suffer for Him…"* **Philippians 1:27-30**

Be on your guard; stand firm in the faith; be courageous; be strong. Do everything in love (1 Cor 16:13-14)….

ARISE, SHINE AND BE COUNTED AMONG THE WARRIOR CLASS OF THE LORD!